Music of the Renaissance

Music of the Renaissance

Giulio Ongaro

David Brinkman, Advisory Editor

GREENWOOD PRESS
Westport, Connecticut • London

Library of Congress Cataloging-in-Publication Data

Ongaro, Giulio Maria.
   Music of the renaissance / Giulio Ongaro
     p. cm.
   Includes bibliographical references and indexes.
   ISBN 0–313–32263–5 (alk. paper)
    1. Music—15th century—History and criticism. 2. Music—16th century—History and criticism. I. Title.
   ML172.O54 2003
   780′.9′031—dc22   2003047242

British Library Cataloguing in Publication Data is available.

Library of Congress Catalog Card Number: 2003047242
ISBN: 0–313–32263–5

First published in 2003

Greenwood Press, 88 Post Road West, Westport, CT 06881
An imprint of Greenwood Publishing Group, Inc.
www.greenwood.com

Printed in the United States of America

The paper used in this book complies with the
Permanent Paper Standard issued by the National
Information Standards Organization (Z39.48–1984).

10 9 8 7 6 5 4 3 2 1

To my mother

Contents

Acknowledgments

It is nearly impossible to thank all the people who have helped me conduct my research on Renaissance music. I would like to single out the staff at the Archivio di Stato di Venezia, in particular Dr. Michela Dal Borgo, for the assistance generously given to me over many years of visits, and for the many stimulating conversations on historical matters. Grants from the Gladys Krieble Delmas Foundation, from the National Endowment for the Humanities, and from the University of Southern California have helped me conduct my research in European libraries and archives. I am grateful to Andrea Begel, of Art Resource, for her help in finding the illustrations, to Kevin Cooper for the music examples, and to my colleague Dr. Karl Swearingen for his very generous help with various technical issues. Thanks also to David Brinkman and Rob Kirkpatrick for their comments and suggestions and to the staff at Greenwood Press for their help. My students at the University of Southern California have often made me question my own assumptions and have caused me to think more clearly about many of the topics I discuss in the book. I owe a debt in particular to my teaching assistants, whose thoughts and ideas I have always found to be stimulating and thought provoking. Finally, I owe an even bigger debt to my family, particularly to my wife Cheryl, who continues to support my self-indulgent fascination with music history with great sense of humor and love.

Any errors and inaccuracies are, of course, my own.

A Basic Chronology
of the Renaissance and
Renaissance Music

ca. 1390–1453 Lifetime of John Dunstable, the "fount and origin" of a new musical style, according to the later theorist Johannes Tinctoris. Dunstable and Leonel Power (d. 1445) are the two most important composers of the so-called English School of the early Renaissance.

1417 The Council of Constance ends the Papal Schism, a period begun in 1378, when two, and later three, rival popes claimed the throne of Peter. Martin V elected Pope.

1431 Death of Joan of Arc.

1436 The church of Santa Maria del Fiore in Florence, a marvel of contemporary architecture because of the huge dome built by the architect Brunelleschi, is dedicated in a ceremony witnessed by Pope Eugenius IV, with music by Guillaume Dufay.

1400–1474 Lifetime of Guillaume Dufay, the greatest composer of his generation. A cosmopolitan composer, Dufay worked in Italy and in his native France and gained wide fame for his music.

1453 Fall of Constantinople (modern day Istanbul) to the Ottoman Turks. Many scholars flee to Europe, bringing manuscripts still unknown to the West. Knowledge of Classical Greek increases in the West thanks to this influx, stimulating an exploration of Greek writings on music.

ca. 1454	Gutenberg prints his Bible from movable type.
ca. 1410–1497	Lifetime of Johannes Ockeghem. Ockeghem, who spent most of his career at the court of France, was the most influential composer of his generation and, at his death, was mourned by many younger composers who considered him their master, either because they had studied directly with him or because they used his music as a model.
1446–1506	Lifetime of Christopher Columbus.
ca. 1450–1521	Life of Josquin Desprez, called by some the "prince of musicians." Josquin was born in France but spent a considerable part of his career in Italy. He was greatly admired by his contemporaries, among them Martin Luther, who considered him the "master of the notes."
1469–1492	Rule of Lorenzo de Medici, "the Magnificent," in Florence. A period of great patronage of the arts in the Italian city, which attracts musicians, artists, and writers.
1477	Death of Charles the Bold, Duke of Burgundy, and end of the independence of his Duchy.
1485	Richard III defeated at the battle of Bosworth by Henry Tudor, who assumes the throne of England with the name of Henry VII.
ca. 1485–1525	Heyday of the frottola. This courtly Italian song adopted simple melodies and tuneful accompaniments, together with down-to-earth texts, to imitate popular music. It was particularly cultivated in northern Italy, especially in Ferrara and Mantua.
1492	Columbus lands in the Americas.
1492	Ferdinand and Isabella, king and queen of Spain, conquer Granada, the last bastion of Moorish (Muslim) presence on the Iberian peninsula, and unify the country under their rule. The Jews are also expelled from Spain or forced to convert to Catholicism.
1494	Aldus Manutius establishes his publishing business in Venice. His editions of the classics, especially of Greek books, are considered one of the most impor-

	tant contributions to the intellectual life of the Renaissance.
1501	The first book of music printed from movable type, adapting the invention of Gutenberg, is published in Venice by the printer Ottaviano dei Petrucci da Fossombrone. It is printed using a technically complex process that makes it relatively expensive and time-consuming.
1503	Leonardo da Vinci paints the *Mona Lisa*.
1505	Martin Luther enters a monastery.
1509–1547	Rule of Henry VIII in England. Although he is perhaps most famous for his six wives and for breaking with the Church of Rome, Henry was also a music lover, an eager dancer in his youth, and perhaps also a composer, since a few pieces attributed to him can be found in English manuscripts of the time.
1513	Michelangelo completes the ceiling of the Sistine Chapel in Rome.
1513–1521	Papacy of Leo X, one of the most important patrons of the arts in Renaissance Italy.
1517	Martin Luther posts his 95 theses, thus setting in motion the events that will lead to the Protestant Reformation.
1527	Sack of Rome by Imperial troops. Many artists and musicians active in the city flee to other locations, with great positive consequences for the intellectual and artistic life of many other cities.
1527	The Flemish composer Adrian Willaert (d. 1562) moves to Venice, where he becomes one of the most respected musicians and teachers of the time. His style is codified by one of his students, the theorist Gioseffo Zarlino, and is taken as a model by the subsequent generation of composers.
1527	Pierre Attaingnant prints his first book of French songs using a new and improved system of printing that in a short time becomes the standard for the industry. Attaingnant thus makes possible the great expansion of music printing in the sixteenth century.

1530   Charles V is crowned Holy Roman Emperor by Pope
               Clement VII.

ca. 1530–1594 Lifetime of the Franco-Flemish composer Orlando di
               Lasso. One of the true cosmopolitan composers of
               the century, Lassus worked in Italy and Belgium be-
               fore being hired by the court of the Archduke of
               Bavaria in 1556. He remained in Munich until his
               death, becoming *maestro di cappella* (director of
               music) in 1563. Lassus composed in all styles of
               sacred and secular music of the time, becoming one
               of the most popular and prolific composers.

1541   The poet Clément Marot translates the psalms into
               French.

1542   The Roman Inquisition is established.

1543   The astronomer Copernicus publishes *De revolutionibus
               orbium coelestium* ("On the Orbits of Celestial Bodies"),
               questioning the medieval assumptions about the cos-
               mos.

1545–1563   Council of Trent. The Catholic Church convenes this
               council to fight the tide of Protestantism. The Council
               of Trent attempts to reform sacred music, recommend-
               ing that music convey pious sentiments and text be un-
               derstandable by the listeners. It also condemns the
               practice of using secular melodies within sacred pieces.

1546   Death of Martin Luther.

1547   Death of Francis I, king of France. Death of Henry
               VIII; his son Edward VI became king of England.

1551   Giovanni Pierluigi da Palestrina, considered by later
               generations to be the epitome of the composer of
               Catholic church music, begins his service at the papal
               court.

1553   Death of Edward VI, king of England. Queen Mary,
               daughter of Henry VIII and Catherine of Aragon,
               takes the throne.

1555   Queen Mary abolishes all religious laws passed by her
               predecessors Henry VIII and Edward VI, thus return-
               ing England to the Catholic faith.

1558	Queen Mary dies. The rule of Queen Elizabeth begins in England. The Queen reestablishes the Church of England.
1559	The treaty of Cateau-Cambrésis sanctions the predominance of Spain in Italian affairs.
1559	The *Index of Prohibited Books* is established by the Catholic Church.
1570	The Turkish fleet occupies the island of Cyprus, in the Eastern Mediterranean, a possession of the Republic of Venice.
1571	At the battle of Lepanto, off the Greek coast, a fleet of Western European nations defeats the Turkish fleet and checks temporarily Turkish naval power and expansion. Lepanto is celebrated in the arts and literature, especially in Venice, whose fleet has a central role in the victory.
1572	Massacre of St. Bartholomew. French Protestants (Huguenots) are seized and massacred by the royal forces.
1573–92	At the house of Count Giovanni de' Bardi, in Florence, spirited debates on music help shape a new musical style, which will be fully developed in the following century.
1577	Pope Gregory XIII orders Palestrina and his colleague Annibale Zoïlo to supervise the reform of the books of Gregorian chant, the official liturgical music of the Catholic Church.
1581	Vincenzo Galilei, a professional musician and the father of the scientist Galileo, publishes his *Dialogue on Ancient and Modern Music*, advocating a solo style of singing and rejecting the polyphony then prevalent.
1588	Defeat of the Armada by the English fleet.
1588	Nicholas Yonge publishes *Musica transalpina*, a collection of Italian madrigals translated into English.
1594	Shakespeare writes *Romeo and Juliet*.
1594	Death of Palestrina and Lasso.

1597   *Dafne,* the "first" opera, is performed at the court in
              Florence. The music does not survive.

1600   *Euridice,* the first surviving opera, is performed in
              Florence.

The Renaissance: An Introduction to the Historical Period

WHAT IS THE RENAISSANCE?

In music, when we speak of the historical period known as the Renaissance we generally mean the time from about 1425 to 1600, although these chronological limits might vary in other disciplines. The term itself was coined in the nineteenth century, well after the end of this historical period, but it seems to embody a feeling widely shared in the fifteenth and sixteenth centuries that a new age had arrived signaling a rebirth (the literal meaning of Renaissance) of classical learning. The term was not immediately applied to music, particularly since the history of music in the Renaissance does not seem to fit the concept of rebirth. Renaissance scholars could study newly rediscovered texts by ancient Greek and Roman authors and philosophers, and visual artists studied Greek and Roman models, but Renaissance musicians could not point to antiquity as a model because they lacked any practical knowledge of Greek or Roman music. Nevertheless, Renaissance music followed the path of other intellectual pursuits by entering into an era of significant changes and innovations.

In any historical period, the history of the arts is influenced by many nonartistic developments in fields such as politics, economics, religion, and technology. Although we might think that the arts are relatively independent of such influences, and more dependent on the inspiration of the individual artist, in fact the arts always respond to the demands and pressures of the society in which they develop, and this is particularly true of Renaissance music. The Renaissance was a period of great intellectual growth, of scientific advancements, of turmoil and

achievements. We all know at least some of the events that occurred
during this period. Some seemingly important events had little direct
influence on music in the Renaissance, while others, perhaps less important in society as a whole, affected music more deeply. For example,
one of the most important events of this period is without a doubt
the discovery of the Americas and the beginning of their colonization
by Europeans, yet the effects of such a momentous event were not
greatly felt in music. We can say that the primary way in which music
was affected by the discovery was that Spain, among other countries,
now began to receive large revenues from the new lands, thereby allowing the Emperor of Spain to devote more money to activities such
as the patronage of music. In general, though, this event cannot be
considered among the most important of the Renaissance with regard
to music. On the other hand, the fall of Constantinople to the
Ottoman Turks in 1453, less important in the long run than the
discovery of the Americas, began a chain of events that had deep repercussions in music, as we shall see later.

It is then absolutely necessary to begin our journey into Renaissance
music by discussing first the general factors that helped shape music
in the Renaissance so that we gain a better understanding of all aspects of the role and development of music in Renaissance society.

CHRONOLOGICAL BOUNDARIES

Any type of subdivision of the history of music into separate chronological periods is somewhat arbitrary. The chronological boundaries we
choose for any of these periods are often established long after the fact
by historians and might not have seemed so clear-cut to contemporaries. It is normal for historians to concentrate on new developments that
we see as defining moments of an era, but we have to keep in mind
that, even when these occurred, old styles and ways of making music
did not disappear suddenly and that, in fact, the coexistence of old and
new is a normal situation in the arts. We should also remember that
the boundaries of the Renaissance have been set differently in different
disciplines: For some historians of literature and visual arts the Renaissance began in the fourteenth century, but for music we have traditionally set the beginning of the Renaissance in the first half of the fifteenth
century. The exact date has been somewhat flexible, but to set it at
around 1425 is a good compromise. In this we are helped by one of
the most important theorists of the late fifteenth century, the Flemish

Johannes Tinctoris who wrote around 1476: "In addition, it is a matter of great surprise that there is no composition written over forty years ago which is thought by the learned to be worthy of performance."[1] This is an incredibly blunt statement worthy of some consideration. It is as if some music critic today declared that no classical music composed before 1960 is worth hearing, cutting out Bach, Mozart, Beethoven, Brahms, and all the other masters whose music fills the programs of every symphony orchestra. Tinctoris, however, was an astute observer of music in his time, and he identified the music of the English composers active up to about 1450 as the beginning of a new musical style. Indeed, when we look at the music of English composers such as Leonel Power (d. 1445) and John Dunstable (d. 1453), we notice that it has features not previously seen in Western European art music. In particular this music, written in a distinctive style called by contemporaries the "English countenance," is full of consonant harmonies, so much so that the word most often used to describe it in the fifteenth century is "sweetness," and it does represent a major break with previous musical styles. It is appropriate then that we agree with Tinctoris and set the beginning of the Renaissance at around 1425, when both Power and Dunstable were active as composers.

The ending date for the Renaissance period is usually given as 1600, which coincides with the performance of the first surviving musical opera. This date is a bit more problematic: Some early seventeenth-century commentators traced the beginning of something new to a point about a generation earlier, around 1575. Nevertheless, we can say that the whole period from about 1575 to 1625 is full of creative innovations and intense debates about music and its aesthetics, which influenced music for centuries, and thus 1600 is a somewhat reasonable final term for the Renaissance in music.

THE POLITICAL LANDSCAPE OF RENAISSANCE EUROPE

In the Renaissance the political map of Europe was quite different from what it is today. Large sections of the continent were not unified into national states, while others had developed into larger countries similar to those of today. The trend was certainly toward larger units, and it was during the Renaissance, for example, that Spain, France, and, to a lesser extent, England developed into countries of a size more or less equivalent to that of their modern counterparts.

If we look at the map of Europe in approximately 1425, we immediately notice the differences: Spain is not yet a unified country, and there is still a Moorish Muslim kingdom around Granada; France is smaller than today, with a large part of its northern territories under English occupation and with an important state, the duchy of Burgundy, carved out of its eastern borders; Belgium and the Netherlands are not unified countries but a collection of semi-independent cities; Italy is split into a variety of states large and small; and Germany lacks a unified identity.

Much of the rest of Europe was divided into smaller political subdivisions; sometime even areas nominally under the control of a monarch were in fact semi-independent. The most famous example of this practice can be found in the fifteenth-century duchy of Burgundy, a loosely assembled territory roughly between modern-day France and Germany, whose dukes theoretically owed allegiance to the King of France (to whom they were related) but, in fact, acted as independent rulers, even allying themselves with the long-time enemies of France, the English kings. The type of centralized government that we find later in European history was not entirely in place even in larger political units, and the situation allowed cities and small sections of territory under royal or imperial authority to carve out a measure of independence with relatively tenuous links to the central government. Even subjects of a centralized state could be defiant toward the royal authority. When King Philip II of Spain tried to commandeer Catalonian workers to help in building his battle fleet, they answered bluntly: "The people of Catalonia, by the liberties they have been granted are not like those of Toledo [i.e., of the Castilian region] where any constable can order carpenters to be brought by force. Here Your Majesty is seen as an individual in a contract."[2]

The large number of smaller states had a profound effect on the arts, perhaps nowhere else as obviously as in Italy. The Italian peninsula was divided into a patchwork of states large and small, and an Italian from Milan, for example, when referring to "foreigners" could as easily be talking about Florentines as Germans. In the south of Italy there was a larger political unit, the Kingdom of Sicily, which extended from Naples to the island of Sicily and was under a foreign dynasty, but the north and the center of the peninsula were divided into many states and city-states. Almost all of these supported a court whose ruler was in a state of constant competition with his (or, more rarely, her) fellow rulers. This competition took the form of traditional political struggles, from diplomatic offensives to actual war, but it had an important component that was active at all times. Renaissance rulers felt they were judged not only on their prowess in war and in the administration of a state but also on their magnificence and generosity in courtly life. Thus an important element of government was to spend considerable amounts of money on architectural projects, paintings, sculptures, and in the patronage of literary figures, artists, and musicians. It is not unusual in this period to see an important ruler writing personal letters to the ruler of a rival court to ask for the services of a musician or artist employed there, and the competition generated by these attitudes meant that there were real opportunities for the best musicians to get higher salaries and better working conditions. In 1520 the Venetian government loaned a musician to the pope.

The instrumentalist Giovanni Maria (or, in Venetian dialect, Zuan Maria), a virtuoso on wind instruments, was allowed by the Venetian government, which employed him, to travel to Rome for the period of one year following a request by Pope Leo X. The document was signed by the ruler of Venice, the Doge, and his counselors. Notice the type of pressure placed on the Venetian government to comply: Venice, recovering from a long, difficult war could hardly afford to antagonize the pope.

June 15, 1520

Leonardo Loredan, by the grace of God Doge of Venice. We wish to disclose to all who will read this letter that we are always willing to please in all things His Holiness, the Pope Leo X, because of the obedience that we owe him, so that we desire to satisfy his wishes with a happy disposition, such as his strong desire, which we have learned from the letters of our ambassador in Rome and of His Holiness, the Pope himself, that we should grant him the services of our trumpet player Giovanni Maria, a request that was also repeated to us and reiterated in person by the Reverend Lord Altobello Averoaldo, Bishop of Pola, and Papal ambassador, in the name of the Holy Pontiff mentioned above. For which reasons we allowed, and we allow by the present letter that the said Giovanni Maria should be able to throw himself at the feet of the Pope, so that he could render his services there for the period of one year, and without losing his job of trumpeter for our government.[3]

There were, of course, positive and negative factors both in large states and in the smaller political units. Larger states could mobilize much larger resources and, thus, offer a more splendid court life, but the centralization seen in these states could also be detrimental to competition. In late sixteenth-century England, for example, London and the court of Queen Elizabeth were by far the most important centers of music. That meant that the fashion of the court and the personal taste of the sovereign had a major influence on artistic developments and that artists not connected with the court and not protected and encouraged by the Queen had less of a chance to become successful and well paid. Smaller states might not have been able to compete on the level of overall resources, but their proliferation made it possible for artists to have a relatively high number of employment opportunities within a small geographical area. In northern Italy, for example, the existence of several splendid smaller states (among them Milan, Mantua, Ferrara, Venice, and Florence) within the space of a few hundred miles created a climate of competition that favored musicians and artists.

Of great influence on artistic developments were also the numerous conflicts and wars of this period. Many of these effects were not confined to artists, of course. When the Imperial troops took Rome in 1527 and proceeded to go on a rampage for several days in the city killing, raping and pillaging, musicians and artists were not more affected than the rest of the population. Still, what had been a center of the arts under Pope Leo X (d. 1521) lost a number of literary and artistic figures who in the wake of the sack of the city decided to move to safer places. Wars and epidemics could turn a flourishing region into an area struggling for survival and, thus, less likely to devote large resources to nonessential activities such as music. For example, the duchy of Milan, certainly one of the most splendid courts of the fifteenth century and host to the great Leonardo da Vinci (who was an amateur musician of considerable skill), lost its independence in the warfare and invasions of the late fifteenth century, and its capital never recovered the leading role in the arts that it had enjoyed in its heyday.

HUMANISM

The most important intellectual movement in the Renaissance is, without a doubt, humanism. The term does not imply, as some have wrongly assumed, a move away from religion or God but implies a different relationship with the world and with God. The term comes from the concept of the *studia humanitatis* (a term that could be rendered as "studies of human things" or "studies of civilization") denoting those intellectual pursuits that did not revolve around theological and religious concerns. Humanists were primarily scholars who were interested in a revival of ancient Greek and Roman learning and who began to look at a variety of questions with a more skeptical and pragmatic eye. In literary studies, for example, humanists began the tradition of textual criticism that continues to this day. Humanists on the whole were not against religion, but they thought that other subjects were also worthy of study. Starting in Italy and slowly spreading to the rest of Europe, humanism reinvigorated Western European thought, encouraged people to question old assumptions, and created a new ideal of the perfect gentleman and lady. The ideal included education as a central component, and humanists established palace schools at many important courts, teaching not only the children of the nobility but also sometimes young boys from middle or lower classes who had shown an aptitude for learning. A big boost to humanistic studies was given by a new interest in the Greek language, spurred by the exodus of Greek-speaking scholars who abandoned the last bastion of the old Eastern Roman Empire when Constantinople (modern-day Istanbul) was overrun by the Ottoman Turks in 1453. Fluency in Greek had been somewhat rare among Western European scholars, but after 1453 it spread rapidly thanks to the influence of these exiles, and by the late sixteenth century it was relatively common among intellectuals. This enabled scholars to read Greek authors in the original instead of relying on texts that had often been Latin translations of Arabic translations of the Greek originals. The exiles fleeing the Turkish advance also brought with them books from antiquity that had not been known to the West. In pursuits as varied as the sciences, philosophy, theater, literature, and music, this new knowledge encouraged theoretical debates and practical experimentation and changed the development of these disciplines.

The most important direct influences of humanism on music can be summarized as follows: First, by perfecting a new ideal of the cultivated and sophisticated aristocrat who should be able to write poetry and sing songs as easily as lead armies into battle, it encouraged music as a pastime, both for the aristocrats and for the larger class of well-to-do non-nobles who began to imitate the manners of the nobility. By the second half of the sixteenth century, having some musical ability was considered important to be successful in polite society as music took on an important social function. As the aristocracy moved from its country estates and castles to urban courts, the skills most necessary changed from those required for hunting and warfare to those needed for survival at a sophisticated court, where a skill such as facility in writing clever poems could mean increased access to, and friendship with, the ruler. During this period it became absolutely necessary for any ruler or important nobleman to be seen also as a patron of the arts. While this had been more or less true for centuries, by the late fifteenth century this meant, among other things, paying for a growing musical establishment at court, thus creating more and better employment opportunities for musicians.

Secondly, humanism focused much theoretical debate on music. Ancient Greek authors discussed at considerable length the effects (both positive and negative) of music in society, and Renaissance humanists sought to re-create those effects. They studied what the ancient authors had written about music and arrived at a variety of solutions that, in their opinion, recaptured the power of music described by the ancient philosophers. Some of these solutions involved the relationship of music and words, while others concentrated on arcane theoretical debates about such matters as the proper mathematical subdivision of musical intervals. Particularly in the field of the relationship of text and music, these debates were important because they actually stimulated practicing composers to experiment with ways to write music that better expressed the sentiments and emotions of the text. In a bit of generalization, we could say that the whole history of vocal music in the Renaissance is the history of a continuous search for more expressive solutions. Earlier periods had not been always interested in the expression of the text in music. Some late medieval musical manuals even suggest writing a complete musical composition before trying to fit the text in "as best as one can." As we shall see, this change of attitude had major implications for the development of Renaissance music.

In short, humanism brought an entirely new attitude that influenced a variety of fields, and music was not immune from these important influences.

TECHNOLOGICAL DEVELOPMENTS: MUSIC PRINTING

One of the most important technological developments of the Renaissance was Gutenberg's invention, of a system to print books from movable type. Within a few decades printing presses were used to feed the appetite of a public imbued with humanistic ideals. Specialized presses, such as that of Aldus Manutius in Venice, turned out book after book in Latin and Greek, making the classics available to a much larger public than ever before. At the turn of the century, a system for the printing of music was first devised, and the public, now encouraged to be more musically literate, began to buy music in quantities that would have been unthinkable a few years earlier. Again, the influence of this development on musical taste, on the working conditions of composers and musicians, and on the economics of music was considerable and probably comparable to that of the introduction of recorded sound in the twentieth century. As music became accessible to a larger public, composers began to consider public taste and not just the preferences of a monarch in their production of music. Some composers became real "stars": many younger musicians would later claim (whether it was true or not) to have been their students, and theorists used their music as an example of the correct style of composition. Although income from the sale of music books was not sufficient to support a composer, it became for some a sizable amount, enough to influence the way they pursued their profession. In short, the fallout from the invention of music printing was wide ranging and had substantial effects on Renaissance music.

SOCIAL DEVELOPMENTS

One very important social development in the Renaissance was the growth, both in terms of demographics and of power, of an urban middle class. The social group that stood between the aristocracy and the lower classes took an increasingly important role in the economic, social, and political life of Europe. For music and other arts the growth of this social class meant an increase in the opportunities to benefit financially from a career in the arts. The middle classes, now with more money and more leisure time to fill, began to look at the behavioral models presented by the nobility and to take part in those activities that would mark them as being cultivated and sophisticated. It became more and more acceptable for wealthy commoners to arrange marriages with members of the nobility, and their lifestyle became practically indistinguishable from that of the aristocracy. This tendency was codified in Giovanni della Casa's 1558 manual of behavior, *Il Galateo*, a book meant to teach the middle classes the behavior that was learned by the nobility from a very early age.

This excerpt from Il Galateo *by Monsignor Giovanni della Casa, a treatise on everyday manners, was written between 1552 and 1555, and published in 1558. It is meant to teach proper behavior in society. Della Casa does not focus only on small details of manners as he tries to set the standards for civilized behavior.*

Some people have an awful habit of putting their hands on any part of their body whenever they feel like it. Also, a polite gentleman will not get ready to deal with his natural needs in front of others, nor, being done with those, will he get dressed in their presence. I will not allow that when one blows his nose, he will open the handkerchief and look inside, as if expecting to find there rubies and pearls brought out from the inside of his skull.

    Do not offer to someone else the glass from which you have been drinking, unless that person is a very close friend; and it is even less appropriate that you should give to someone else a pear or other fruit from which you have already taken a bite. Similarly, there are noises annoying to the ear, such as the grinding of teeth, whistling, screeching, rubbing stones together, and scratching on metal, and one should abstain from all these activities whenever possible. And not only that, but one should not be singing, particularly as a soloist, if he has a voice that is rough and out of tune; very few follow this precept, and in fact it seems that those who have less aptitude [for singing] are those who do it more often. And do not think that all these rules I gave you above are unimportant, because even the lightest blows can kill a person, if he receives too many of them.[4]

This desire to behave in a cultivated manner had important repercussions for music. Members of the middle class bought music manuals that promised to teach them how to become proficient in music, bought more music books and more musical instruments, took more music lessons than ever before, and learned how to dance the latest dances. Certain musical activities that might have been restricted in the past to a relatively small elite were now available to a much larger group. Members of the middle classes also tended to gather in groups that ranged from religious confraternities to private academies to guilds and trade groups. These groups, with their collective economic power, made it possible for many members of the middle classes to be part of the patronage system in a way that had been reserved traditionally only for the nobility. The urbanization of society, of course, also disrupted traditional patterns. Even as late as 1500 only four cities in Europe had more than one hundred thousand inhabitants: Venice, Naples, Paris, and Constantinople. It is in this period, though, that the urban population began a considerable growth spurt, leading to a doubling of the population by the year 1600 in cities such as Rome, Vienna, Nuremberg, and Hamburg; a three-fold increase in Lisbon and Seville; and an incredible quadrupling of the population in London between 1509 and 1600.[5] This was happening even as much of Europe remained relatively thinly inhabited, strikingly different from the bustling, growing cities.

Inhabitants of the cities had more access to the tools of leisure, such as books or musical instruments, and also had a much better chance of being exposed to musical performances not available in rural areas. For example, the urban dweller who went to the local cathedral on a special feast day would be able to hear a great choir singing music by some of the best composers of the time, whereas his rural counterpart might only be able to hear very simple music perhaps performed in a less-than-satisfactory way. There seems to be also a growing gap between city and country, with the country folk often used as the butt of jokes for the entertainment of the middle class and aristocracy. Some of the most important plays of the early sixteenth century in Italy, for example those written by the Paduan Angelo Beolco, who was better known as Ruzzante, have at their center characters portraying peasants shown as being cowardly, cuckolded, wily, untrustworthy, and simple minded. In conclusion, the social changes in this period combined with other advancements to stimulate the production and consumption of music to a degree previously unknown on the European continent. We can say without exaggeration that the musical landscape of 1600 was drastically different from that of the beginning of the Renaissance.

RELIGIOUS TURMOIL

Another very important factor in the development of music was the momentous change in the religious landscape of Western Europe. The Renaissance began with a Europe that was more or less unified under the pope. Even though the papacy had been battered by the events of the period between the fourteenth and fifteenth centuries, when first two, then three, popes laid claims to the throne of Peter by involving most of Europe in a game of religious and political alliances, the fifteenth century brought a ray of hope when the Schism was recomposed and a single pope began to rebuild the church. Following that troublesome period, many voices were raised in favor of significant religious reforms in the fifteenth century, but the failure to implement any of the changes proposed opened the door for a much more traumatic set of events in the early sixteenth century. In general we can say that even before the reforms of Martin Luther, people in many parts of Europe supported religion but were openly critical of the Catholic Church and of its clergy. It has been estimated that the clergy, including monks and nuns, numbered between one and three percent of the total population. Many were dedicated and educated individuals with a deep commitment to their mission, but many were also poorly educated and poorly trained, pushed into a profession without feeling a real calling. Many bishops and abbots behaved like secular rulers, and the population of Europe was also resentful of the amount of money that went into the coffers of the church, an act that was seen as taking wealth from one's region in order to give it to the papal court in Rome. One example, and one which Luther condemned strongly, was the practice of selling indulgences, that is, total or partial reductions in the time the soul of the deceased would spend in Purgatory before reaching Heaven. This practice flourished in the fifteenth century, as the Church tried to gather money to recover from the turmoil of the previous period, and was instrumental in creating a huge amount of hostility among the masses.

The lack of an internal reform of the Catholic Church made it possible for religious reforms to be successful in the sixteenth century. Pioneered by Martin Luther in Germany, the Reformation expanded its influence on large areas of the continent. By the late sixteenth century many areas of Europe had moved from the Catholic Church to one of the reformed religions, changing the religious structure of Europe. More importantly for music, religious reforms often also meant changes in the way services were conducted, including possible changes in sacred music performances. In some reformed churches music was seen as inherently dangerous, to be strictly regulated and limited, while others simply changed the type of music from that heard in Catholic churches to fit better into the new services. Just as in the case of painters and sculptors of religious art who were not needed by the unadorned Protestant churches, musicians and composers of sacred music found themselves without a sizable and steady source of income. The Catholic Church, in its effort for an internal reform, also devoted some time to the issue of music, arriving at guidelines that modified the requirements for the music to be heard during the Mass and other services. In sum, religious changes often brought with them changes of a practical nature, for example, in the employment opportunities or working conditions of musicians and in the type of music expected of sacred music composers.

CONCLUSIONS

The 175 years that comprise the Renaissance in music were a time of change in society, of reassessment of long-held beliefs and traditions and of discovery not only in the field of practical and theoretical applications but also in intellectual pursuits. If an early Renaissance European could have been brought back to life around 1600, he or she would have found a lot that would have remained familiar but would have also been astonished at the changes in politics, society, religion, the visual arts, and, of course, music. For example, he or she would have noticed a change from the early fourteenth-century love songs, written for a small elite of noblemen and embodying the ideals of a dying feudal society, to the much larger repertory of secular songs available in a variety of publications that circulated widely all over Europe. The intimate polyphonic pieces for religious services written in the first part of the fifteenth century changed to the large-scale majestic pieces for voices and instruments that could be heard in the late sixteenth century. In this book we will study how these musical developments and the whole music world were changed by the political, social, and religious events of the Renaissance.

NOTES

1. Translated in Johannes Tinctoris, *Liber de arte contrapuncti (On the Art of Counterpoint)*, transl. by A. Seay (Rome: American Institute of Musicology, 1961), 14.

2. Quoted in John Hale, *The Civilization of Europe in the Renaissance* (New York: Atheneum, 1994), 89. Hale's book is a very good introduction to the Renaissance, although it is not organized as a chronological survey of political events.

3. The original of the letter is in the Archivio di Stato di Venezia (Venetian State Archive); the translation is mine.

4. Monsignor Giovanni della Casa, *Galateo, overo de' costumi*, ed. B. Maier (Milano: Mursia, 1971), 35. The translation is mine.

5. Hale, *The Civilization of Europe*, 87.

CHAPTER 1

An Introduction to Renaissance Music

The music of the Renaissance has definitely benefited from the increased general interest in early music in the past few decades. Today the shelves of a good record store carry many more performances of Renaissance music than ever before. Still, it would be an exaggeration to say that most Renaissance music is familiar to a large section of the population or even to a large section of classical music lovers. It is not often played on classical radio stations or heard as part of mainstream classical concerts. Occasionally a piece or two might be sung by a college or high school choir, and there might be a "madrigal dinner" at which a few Renaissance pieces are performed, but those pieces tend to be consistently from a relatively narrow band of the entire Renaissance musical repertory. In short, it cannot be assumed that someone, even an individual with an interest in this period, would be very familiar with the music of the Renaissance and with its defining characteristics. A few of the concepts explained in this chapter might seem too basic to some, while others will undoubtedly seem strange to someone used to hearing classical music from the time of Mozart and Beethoven or twenty-first-century popular music. Nevertheless, a little effort will be very rewarding and will enable the reader to enjoy more fully this wonderful repertory. In order to become more familiar with the music of the Renaissance, in this chapter we are going to examine what musical features define Renaissance music, and we will learn how to distinguish between several styles of Renaissance music.[1]

GENERAL CHARACTERISTICS

Although it is almost impossible to generalize about the music of any historical period, there are a few generalizations that we can apply to Renaissance music.

First, the musical compositions of the Renaissance tend to be shorter than the pieces of classical music heard in a modern concert hall. Many pieces are about the length of a modern popular song or only slightly longer. Although there are some exceptions, most Renaissance pieces are short enough that a modern listener can easily enjoy them without getting lost in complex musical forms.

Second, most of the surviving music was meant for voices, whether accompanied or unaccompanied. Although instrumental music came of age in this period, the voice still occupied a preeminent place in this repertory. We can say that a majority of the surviving music from the Renaissance was written for combinations of three to five vocal parts without instrumental accompaniment. This might mean that only one singer to a part was needed, producing a kind of intimate setting, or that two or three singers to a part would suffice to fill a choir. Renaissance instrumental music employed instruments that, for the most part, are not part of a standard modern orchestra or band; furthermore, instrumental groups were not as standardized in their composition as they are today. Western Europe had to wait until the seventeenth century, in the Baroque period, to see a standard string orchestra emerge.

Third, to modern ears, most Renaissance music sounds very pleasant, as it seems to avoid combinations of sound that we would describe as "harsh" or "rough." We will see later why composers wrote music in this style, but the important part is that the overall effect on a modern listener may be one of an unrelentingly pleasant and somewhat ethereal sound.

Fourth, most Renaissance music does not have a strong rhythmic beat (unlike modern popular music), and when a clear beat is present it might seem much less definite to modern listeners than that of most other types of music. Composers did use rhythm in very effective ways but, for the most part, without the kind of clear rhythmic pulse that we find, for example, in the music of Bach, Vivaldi, Mozart, or Beethoven. The direct, pounding beat that has become the hallmark of modern pop music was not part of the Renaissance style. Thus, in general, we have to be aware of the subtle uses of rhythm in Renaissance compositions: one exception is in dance music, where a clearer beat was necessary for the dancers who had to execute the various prescribed steps. Also, as we shall see later, the speed of most pieces of Renaissance music (what musicians call "tempo") is not indicated in scores and would have been left up to performers. Occasional remarks by Renaissance writers tend to give us only generic indications, and for the most part the tempo of modern performances of Renaissance music is the result of the educated guess made by performers trained in that particular type of music.

Fifth, Renaissance music is similar to more recent music in that there is no unified mood or feeling in the repertory as a whole. Some pieces (for example, most sacred music) will sound solemn, while other pieces might sound fast, light, and breezy. However, trying to guess at the meaning of a piece of Renaissance music based on how it sounds to us might be problematic because of some of the differences in style. Composers of the Renaissance, just like more modern composers, also introduced sudden changes of mood in a piece to underline a change of imagery in the text or simply to create a musical contrast that would surprise and please the listener.

By now it should be obvious that the one generalization we can make about Renaissance music is that, far from being musically homogeneous, the musical landscape of the period from approximately 1425 to 1600 is made up of a variety of musical expressions. A music lover in Renaissance Europe would have been able to hear music ranging from single vocal melodies without accompaniment to pieces for one or two voices and accompaniment, to settings of sacred or secular texts for four or five distinct vocal parts, to sacred pieces with eight to twelve vocal parts accompanied by an instrumental group. The larger orchestral and choral forces we see in more recent classical music would have been unknown to the Renaissance, but within the ranges previously mentioned, there could be tremendous creativity in forging different and interesting combinations of performers.

CHALLENGES FOR MODERN PERFORMERS

A performer of classical music who specializes in more traditional classical music, such as that played by symphony orchestras today, expects to be told by the musical score many important details about the performance, such as the speed of a piece, the instrumental or vocal combinations needed, whether it is to be played softly or loudly, and so on. The intangible factor that we call interpretation allows performers to deviate slightly from the indications in a score in order to create a more personal performance in the same way that we expect two Shakespearean actors to come up with different performances of the same monologue. Also, some minute details of the performance, for example slight variations in speed meant to give dramatic intensity to a phrase, cannot be notated precisely, and in these cases the composer relies on the skills and knowledge of the performers. In general, however, the modern performer feels that by following the score he or she is re-creating the intentions of the composer.

In a typical Renaissance score performers are given much greater freedom to decide not only slight nuances but also basic elements that can deeply affect the performance. Scores of Renaissance music contain only the basic musical material and, even then, with a fair amount of ambiguity. Generally, only the notes and the meter (the designation of the basic rhythmic pulse) are set down on paper, while all other aspects necessary for a performance are left up to the performer.

Renaissance performers needed to be intimately acquainted with the "rules" to know how to perform a piece correctly. They needed to make decisions as basic as how fast a piece would go, how soft or loud each phrase should sound, who exactly should play or sing a particular piece, how each phrase of music should be interpreted, and so forth.

A typical Renaissance manuscript or print of music looks fairly bare to us, lacking all kinds of musical indications we expect to see from the composer. The illustration on p. 19 shows a page from the first book of polyphonic music printed from movable type published in Venice by the printer Ottaviano dei Petrucci in the first decade of the sixteenth century. This is a vocal piece with the French title "Adieu, mes amours" ("Goodbye, My Loves"). Only the soprano and tenor parts are shown here while the alto and bass are on the facing page. This system, with parts presented separately on the page rather than all together as in a modern orchestral score, is the preferred way of printing music in the Renaissance. The printer has not included the text of the song beyond its title. Perhaps he was doubtful that his Italian public would be interested in the French words, or he did not have a copy of the music with the words. The composer is indicated at the top, right above the music. The name "Josquin" means he is Josquin Desprez (d. 1521), perhaps the most famous composer of the day.

The note shapes look a little strange because they are diamond shaped rather than round, but are otherwise similar to notes found on a modern score. Notice, though, that very little else is given. The top voice is not labeled "soprano" (that would be assumed by the

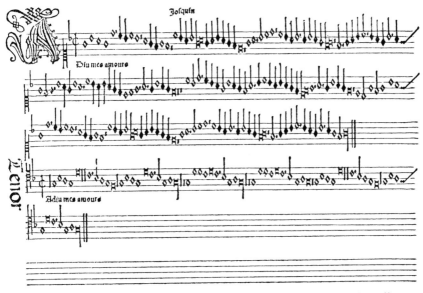

Ottaviano dei Petrucci, a page from his collection *Harmonices musice adhecaton*, first printed in 1501. This page shows the soprano and tenor voices of *Adieu mes amours*, a chanson by Josquin Desprez. (Courtesy of Broude Brothers Limited.)

performer) but sports a fancy initial "A," while the bottom part reads "tenor" in plainer script. No other indication is included in the score anywhere; in fact, the score is even missing bar-lines, those strokes that separate the various rhythmic units in a modern score. It is obvious that the performers would be faced with many choices regarding speed, interpretation, dynamics (the loudness of the piece), and even whether to sing this piece or play it on an instrument.

Although this creates substantial challenges for modern performers, it does not mean that we should despair of ever arriving at a performance that would have been acceptable to Renaissance musicians. Scholars and performers have studied these problems using every possible piece of evidence contained in technical treatises, musical manuals, descriptions of musical performances, comments included in letters, and in visual representations of music making. The result is that we now know a fair amount about the way this music is supposed to sound, though there are plenty of questions that are unanswered. At the same time we should also recognize that there was more flexibility in the performance of Renaissance music than in the classical music of more recent times. One of the disconcerting features of Renaissance music is that sometimes two modern performances of the same piece by different groups might be much more different from each other, for example, than two performances of a Beethoven symphony by different orchestras. In the case of instrumental ensembles, for example, we usually have music written down, for the most part, without any indications of the proper instrumentation. The pragmatic answer is that this often means that any instrument capable of playing a certain part would have been considered appropriate (although with some limitations that we will discuss later). Even vocal music was not necessarily always sung. From documents of the period we know it would have been perfectly acceptable in many situations to have instruments substitute for, or complement, the voices without the need for any indications in the score.

THE SOUND OF RENAISSANCE SINGERS

The actual sound of Renaissance singers is also difficult to re-create. We can say with some confidence that they did not sound at all like modern classically trained singers with their operatic voices. We do know something about the differences, but we really do not know what kind of voice type was preferred, as many descriptions of singing in the period tend to be vague or stop at inconclusive descriptions such as "he sang sweetly" or "it was like the music of the angels." We know that church choirs of the time, for example, were not allowed to employ women singers and that the soprano and alto parts of sacred vocal compositions were usually taken by choirboys, by adult males singing in falsetto or "head voice," or, in the last part of this period, by male castrati, singers who had been emasculated in their youth to preserve their boyhood voices. This feature alone would make a church choir of the Renaissance sound quite different from a modern one. Even the sound of choirboys, which (unlike that of the castrati) is something we can still hear in our century, was probably different. Choirboys often did not reach puberty until relatively late so it was not unusual to encounter a choirboy still singing soprano or alto at the age of sixteen or seventeen when he might have sounded much stronger than a modern, younger boy chorister. Singing in falsetto was a skill in which certain singers specialized, but many singers, even amateurs, could switch between low and high registers when needed. A letter of 1594 describing a gentleman's musical ability states, in part: "As to music, he sings his part by the book in as pleasing a manner as a gentleman [i.e., not a professional musician] can. He has a rather good tenor voice. He also sings the soprano part, but the voice is not so pure in this range, even though graceful."[2] If this seems strange to us, we should remember that, even in popular music of our time, there are many instances of adult males singing high parts in falsetto (almost all the songs of the Beach Boys, for example, have falsetto parts), so we can say that this practice has an unbroken history going back several centuries. Women could, of course, take part in private performances of secular music and were often praised for their singing ability, but their exclusion from the church left them out of a very important repertory of the period. Furthermore, a typical Renaissance church choir would have been relatively small compared with a modern one, and most of the performances would have required only one or two singers to a part, giving the performance a clarity and agility that is often missing when larger choirs attempt the same repertory.

Instruments were also different from those of a symphony orchestra, and there was virtually no "standard" ensemble similar to the modern orchestra so combinations of instruments could be put together in a more flexible manner. Many instruments used in the Renaissance became obsolete after the period, as we will see later, and some of those that survived, such as the flute or the violin, underwent important changes in their construction and playing techniques, so a knowledge of Renaissance instrumentation is essential for a performer of this music.

Far from looking at all these obstacles as problems to be solved through the application of dogmatic rules, it is important to keep an open mind and to realize that this flexibility and variety should be perfectly acceptable and, in fact, desirable. It is possible that, in many cases, performers of the Renaissance were willing to perform the same piece differently each time so that for them there was no "correct" performance that would exclude all other musical solutions.

Again, a parallel with modern music can be made quite easily when we think of the situation that is normal in popular music (including genres such as blues, jazz, and others). In this repertory, we would never ask what is the correct instrumentation for a particular piece or which performance of one song is "correct." Within certain limits we tend to regard all performances as valid and to judge the quality of one particular performance on its own merits.

A TYPICAL AMATEUR PERFORMANCE

Let us imagine a music lover in 1560s Italy, not necessarily a wealthy man but a member of the well-to-do middle class, with sufficient income to spend on music books and music lessons. He has invited his friends for an elaborate dinner followed by musical entertainment, not a concert in the modern sense with professionals playing for a silent audience but a participatory experience where the guests will amuse themselves by playing and singing their favorite music. Typically for the period, guests are not judged to have been properly brought up and educated unless they can sing or play at first sight music that is put before them, so after dinner the host pulls out several music books and encourages his friends to sing some of the newest pieces for four or five voices. Looking at the group he has assembled, he notices that one of the women, the one with the lovely soprano voice, has not shown up, and the gentleman who usually sings bass has a cold. However, this does not mean that the entertainment will have to be canceled. One of the gentlemen is asked to sing the woman's part in falsetto, while the bass singer with a cold picks up an instrument to play the part he was supposed to sing. Such flexibility was typical of private gatherings but even church performances were affected. A group of Italian instrumentalists playing during the course of a church service once found themselves short one member, and they promptly enlisted the services of a choir singer to sing the part intended for the missing instrumentalist. More frequently choirs used instruments to support a section of the choir when needed (for example, if some of the singers were absent) by playing the parts meant for the singers.

In conclusion, it is important, when we listen to modern performances of Renaissance music, to keep in mind that what is presented is almost never the definitive version of a particular piece but simply one of many possible solutions. Instead of searching for an elusive definitive version, we should appreciate the variety and flexibility this music affords the performers.

THE BASICS OF RENAISSANCE MUSICAL STYLE

Texture

The word "texture" in music is commonly used to indicate the way in which a composer puts together the different parts of a composition. For example, we can talk of "thick texture," when a composer writes many different parts playing or singing at the same time, or "thin" texture, when only a few parts are employed. We can also use the term texture to describe the way parts relate to each other. The type of texture that seems to dominate the Renaissance is the one commonly called polyphony (from the Greek, meaning "many sounds"). Generalizing a little bit we can say that one of the characteristics of polyphony is that a composition is made up of separate vocal or instrumental parts, each with its own individuality as a melodic line. Thus, in a piece of polyphony, there is no real "accompaniment," but all voices can be seen as "carrying the tune" at one time or another, and no part is always accompanying. This is very different, for example, from modern popular music in which one voice usually carries the melody, while other voices or, more frequently, instruments are clearly subordinate and accompany the lead singer. Polyphony can be a very democratic texture, allowing each voice or instrument in turn to surge to the front then fade back for a little while, without the concentration on one soloist that we see in other types of music.

In Example 1, we can see a short excerpt from a polyphonic sacred choral work by the composer Josquin Desprez (d. 1521). This is a sec-

Example 1 Josquin Desprez, Pange lingua Mass, Gloria mm. 7–15

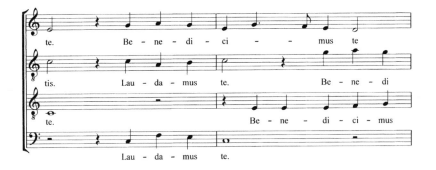

tion of a movement, "Gloria," from one of Josquin's most famous masses. Josquin wrote this movement for four voices, corresponding to soprano, alto, tenor, and bass. Notice in this excerpt how each voice has a distinct melodic shape. We cannot identify any voice as being definitely subordinate to the others. Each part carries a tuneful, separate melody that would make sense as a melody even if heard alone, and the interplay that results from this type of writing adds interest and excitement to the piece. Most vocal (and much instrumental) music of this period uses the same principle although in somewhat different ways. One other feature of this excerpt is that the two top lines, soprano and alto, seem to "follow" one another, each singing the same melody but starting on different notes. This effect is similar to the one found in canons sung everywhere (such as "Row, Row, Row Your Boat"). In musical terms when a polyphonic piece shows this kind of repetition of melodies in different voices the texture is called "imitative polyphony," that is, polyphony that is based on the imitation of melodies by some or all of the voices. Not all polyphony is imitative, but imitative polyphony became the standard for much of the music written from the late fifteenth century to the end of the Renaissance.

Example 2, Andrea Gabrieli's "O sacrum convivium" ("O Sacred Banquet") shows an excerpt that at first sight looks very different from that of example 1. Even in an excerpt like this, though, the composer would be thinking of individual lines so that each part has the same melodic interest as any other part. Notice also that, in the first example, on any given beat the voices will be singing a different syllable of the

Example 2   Andrea Gabrieli, motet "O sacrum convivium," mm. 50–53

text, while in the second excerpt they are all declaiming the text together. In general we would say that the first excerpt, showing clear independence of melodic lines, is in a contrapuntal texture with clear independence of lines; the texture of the second excerpt is sometimes called homophonic (meaning "sounding together") or homorhythmic ("with the same rhythm"). The texture of a great majority of Renaissance pieces falls between these two extremes, with some sections of a work showing a more clearly contrapuntal style and other sections leaning toward homophony, particularly when the composers felt that part of the text needed to be heard clearly.

Not all music of the Renaissance was strictly polyphonic. Although music in three to five parts (whether vocal or instrumental) was the most common, much secular music and quite a bit of instrumental music could be written in such a way that one solo line would stand out from the rest, with other parts clearly limited to an accompaniment. Example 3, a sixteenth-century Spanish secular song known as "romance" (pronounced Ro-MAHN-say) scored for voice and vihuela (a guitar-shaped string instrument popular in Spain), shows one type of texture in which the accompaniment is reduced to little more than strummed chords clearly supporting the vocal line. In instrumental music some standard series of chords were used for accompaniment in a way that is similar to the twelve-bar blues pattern. Some of these became so widely known that they were given nicknames familiar to all musicians of the time; thus, we have generic names such as "passemezzo" (literally, step and a half), "romanesca" (Roman style), or colorful names probably derived from the tunes these patterns originally accompanied, such as "Guardame las vacas" ("Keep an eye on my cows"). Often these patterns were used as the basis for improvisation by a solo instrument. One can imagine that an instrumentalist of the time could have turned to his accompanist and simply asked for a passemezzo or romanesca accompaniment in a particular key and

Example 3   Alonso Mudarra, romance "Triste estava el rey David," mm. 1–5

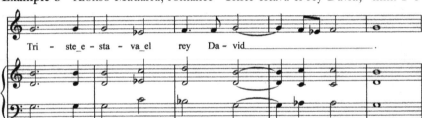

could have known exactly what the accompanist was going to do next, in a way not too different from that of modern performers of jazz or blues.

It goes without saying that melodies without any type of accompaniment could also be heard quite frequently. When we see a melody standing alone we call that texture "monophony" (from the Greek for "one sound"). All of the Gregorian chant heard in churches in the Renaissance and quite a large part of the popular songs were written using this texture. An average person might have heard more monophonic music in his or her lifetime than any other type of music.

Still we cannot deny that polyphony played a major role in Renaissance music and is a constant in the period from 1425 to 1600 so that the entire period has often been called the "Golden Age of Polyphony." On the other hand other musical features, such as melodic and harmonic writing, harmony, and the use of formal patterns of repetition and contrast, changed from one generation to the next. We will examine shortly some of these individual characteristics.

Harmony

In putting together a piece of music, the Renaissance composer had to pay attention to the rules of harmony set down by the theorists of the time. By harmony we mean the effect we hear when two or more musical parts are played or sung together. The study of harmony, that is, of the rules governing how we put various parts together, forms an important part of every musician's training. Generally speaking, hearing two or more notes sound together can give us a sense of rest and satisfaction or make us feel like those two notes don't quite belong together. We call the first type of relationship "consonance" and the second type, "dissonance." Dissonances can be heard on much of twentieth-century classical music, which has contributed to the uneasy feeling that many concert-goers have about that repertory. However, even the most soothing piece of music contains some dissonances. Dissonances create a sense of tension that is resolved to our satisfaction by moving to a consonance. If music did not use any dissonances it would actually sound pretty dull. Different eras have defined what is dissonant in different ways. Dissonance is, thus, to some extent in the ear of the listener. Renaissance music can sound very sweet to our ears not because it does not contain dissonances but because one of the hallmarks of the style is the control of dissonances, that is, in most pieces the use of dissonances is strictly regulated and only introduced in a limited number of situations. As a result we are rarely jolted by some "grating," unexpected sound created by the harmony of the voices singing together. On the other hand, in Renaissance music we often hear harmonies moving in ways a little strange to our ears. Even though most people have not studied harmony in any formal way, we can say that constant exposure to modern music in commercials and film music, for example, shapes their expectations regarding how a piece of music ought to sound. In other words, the average person might not be able to explain why a certain piece does not sound "right," but he or she can tell when something unexpected occurs.

Part of the reason why Renaissance music sometimes sounds somewhat strange to us is that the system of tonality (the set of rules for harmony that is used in most classical music from the seventeenth through the later part of the nineteenth century and the one still used in virtually all popular music of our time) had not yet been established. Renaissance composers were trained in a system, known as the model system, that had been established centuries earlier and was based on melodic patterns known as modes and not on the keys of more modern music. Although it would be easy to regard modes as the equivalent of our modern keys, in effect, a mode behaved quite differently. The two basic differences are (1) modes do not fall into the modern distinction between major and minor keys and (2) pieces written in the modal system sometimes behave in ways that might sound strange to our twenty-first-century ears. For example, a large number of pieces in the Renaissance were composed in Dorian mode, a mode that to us sounds similar to a minor key. In more recent music we usually make an association of major keys as being upbeat and "happy," while the minor keys are often described as "sad." Renaissance composers, though, often used the minor-sounding Dorian mode for pieces that were upbeat, even joyful in character, and it is obvious that for them this mode did not necessarily suggest sadness.

The other feature of modal music that makes it sound somewhat strange to us is that a modal piece does not necessarily end its phrases (that is, cadence) on the "chords" or notes we would expect to hear based on our constant exposure to our own system of keys. The effect to someone who is not acquainted with Renaissance music is sometimes one of surprising endings and perhaps of a sense of unfulfilled expectations, since the music might not behave in the same way as a piece by Mozart or a pop song by the Beatles. Not all Renaissance pieces give us this feeling, however, and some, both vocal and instrumental, sound remarkably modern. Some of the chordal patterns for instrumental improvisation mentioned earlier seem to have a sequence of chords arranged in such a way that they would not be out of place in a modern pop song, while some pieces of vocal polyphony might sound remote to our ears.

THE WRITING OF MELODY AND HARMONY IN RENAISSANCE MUSIC

Melody

The term melody is used in music to indicate a series of notes that are arranged in succession in such a way as to create a recognizable musical unit, belonging together, so to speak. A series of random notes is usually not defined as a melody, since it would lack this basic characteristic. We must keep in mind, though, that musicians from different eras defined what constitutes a "recognizable musical unit" in very different terms: a twentieth-century melody might not have been recognized as such by a fourteenth-century listener. The types of melodies that one encounters in Renaissance music can be widely different depending on the genres, on the specific period, on the style of individual composers, and so forth. Let us consider first the melodic writing in Renaissance sacred pieces, taking as examples pieces from a variety of composers and styles. Sacred music, on the whole, tended to show more uniformity at any given time than the much more fragmented secular music repertoire, and thus it offers us a better model for comparison. Example 4 presents melodic lines written by composers working from the middle of the fourteenth century to the very end of the sixteenth century. The very first melody is actually outside the boundaries of the Renaissance, as it was written by a composer of the late Middle Ages. It is presented here to provide a sense of the contrast between late medieval music and the music of the Renaissance. The melodies are arranged in rough chronological order.

Some differences are immediately apparent. Earlier composers often write melodic lines that seem to be longer and do not have the clear shape that is obvious in later pieces. Also in later melodies, the line will rise and fall largely through a succession of steps (that is, going from one note to the very next one in the scale), while the shape of earlier melodic lines is a little more unpredictable. Later melodies seem

Example 4.1 Guillaume de Machaut, motet "Felix virgo," top voice, mm. 25–33

Que_____ gau - di - um_____ mun - - do_____ tri - sti_____

Example 4.2 John Dunstable, motet "Quam pulcra es," soprano mm. 1–8

Quam_____ pul - cra_____ es, et quam de - -co - ra, ca - ris - si - ma in de - li - - ciis.

Example 4.3 Johannes Ockeghem, Requiem Mass, Offertory, soprano, mm. 1–9

Rex_____ glo - - - - - - - - - - ri - - - ae

Example 4.4 Guillaume Dufay, L'homme armé Mass, Christe, soprano, mm. 6–12

[e] - - - - - - - - lei - son.

Example 4.5   Josquin Desprez, motet "Ave Maria," soprano, mm. 1–12

Example 4.6   Nicolas Gombert, motet "Ave regina caelorum," soprano, mm. 23–31

Example 4.7   Giovanni Pierluigi da Palestrina, motet "Sicut lilium," soprano, mm. 1–11

to be shorter and have a clear sense of form, for example, by surging to a high point and falling back to the note of the beginning. Also later melodies seem to offer short, clear melodic ideas, or motives, that are easily grasped and remembered by the listener, enhancing the sense of clarity of this music. Before we look at these melodies in more detail, let us examine for a moment a very well-known melody that should be familiar to all readers (example 5, "Twinkle Twinkle, Little Star"). In this simple melody we can easily grasp form, since the various segments are short and easily recognizable. The various segments also work in a logical way according to the tonal system with which we are so familiar. Notice how the very first phrase segment ends on a higher note than its beginning, being left hanging there, so to speak, until the second part of the phrase takes us back to the beginning. The effect for us is that we instinctively know that the first phrase segment is not a complete whole. We might not know yet how it is going to end, but we know that this is not a proper ending. Obviously, this is not necessarily the way all music works, but we learn these types of patterns from an early age simply by listening to popular music, soundtracks, commercials, Muzak, and so on. In order to understand the way earlier composers wrote melodies, we have to accept that not all music will follow such simple patterns and that other patterns, harder for us to follow, might be present.

Melody 1 from example 4 is part of a piece by Guillaume de Machaut (d. 1377), perhaps the greatest composer of the late Middle Ages. This is considered to be one of Machaut's later works, when the master was at the peak of his compositional ability, and thus it can be seen as one of the best expressions of the music of this period. One first notices that the melodic writing alternates between repetitive rhythms with short note values and long-held notes. The alternation between these two types of writing seems to occur suddenly and tends to take us by surprise. The range of the melody is rather narrow and it seems to be very simple. This, to be sure, does not mean that Machaut is an "inferior" composer or that he did not know how to write satisfactory melodies. If we were to study the entire piece we would, in fact, notice that he has very cleverly arranged the musical

Example 5 Anonymous, "Twinkle, Twinkle, Little Star"

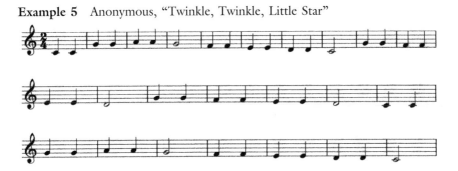

material, creating a large-scale composition that is both impressive and technically superior. It simply means that Machaut was perhaps not interested in some aspects of the melody that became very important to later Renaissance composers.

The second melody comes from one of the pieces often identified as being at the beginning of Renaissance music: "Quam pulcra es" ("How fair art thou"), a setting by John Dunstable (d. 1453) of a Song of Songs text from the Bible. Notice here that the rhythmic values are more homogeneous with less difference between the fastest and the slowest notes. The rhythm of the music respects the accents of the words, most notably in the way Dunstable sets the word "ca-RIS-si-ma" (dearest) shortly after the middle of the musical phrase. The melody also has a very definite shape, rising from C to A and then slowly descending back to C. Toward the end of the phrase (on the word "deliciis") Dunstable writes a melisma, that is, a section where one syllable of the text is set over several notes. This short section prepares us for the end of a musical phrase and the arrival of the rest-ing point (what we call a "cadence"), so when the melody reaches the last C we are expecting it. This is a particularly fine example of the music of the early Renaissance, and, naturally, not all pieces from this period are equally well written. Even in this piece we do notice ex-amples of poor accentuation of words, and the final cadence of this phrase is not prepared as well as one would expect from a later com-poser. Yet this short excerpt shows that Dunstable valued some fea-tures in his melodies that were not as valuable to Machaut and, on the whole, this melody is much more "singable" than the earlier one.

Not all fifteenth-century melodies were as clear-cut as that by Dunstable. In melody 3, we see an example by the great composer Johannes Ockeghem (d. 1497), one of the masters of his generation and the director of music for the court of the King of France. This melody is taken from the Offertory section of the Requiem Mass (the Mass for the Dead) by Ockeghem. You will notice that this melody seems to wander without clear goals and that a clear shape is not im-mediately apparent. Text setting is not an issue here because through-out most of the movement, syllables are held over several notes. All the features contribute to making this melody seem strange to us and less focused than the Dunstable melody. The melody by Ockeghem is relatively peaceful, without the use of fast moving notes (although a faster passage does occur elsewhere in the piece). One other man-ner of melodic writing can be seen in melody 4, a passage from Guillaume Dufay's L'homme armé Mass. This example, as equally "unfocused" as the Ockeghem example, is written in a nervous, lively manner that contrasts with earlier and later sections of the piece. Again, these are features more typical of fifteenth-century music up to about 1475 than of Renaissance music as a whole.

One of the undisputed masters of the period was Josquin Desprez (d. 1521). He represents the "new" style of the late fifteenth and early sixteenth century, a style that saw many changes in melodic and harmonic writing. Melody 5, from his "Ave Maria," is very different from the melodies seen so far. Josquin writes a very simple melody, which is imitated by all voices in turn. The simplicity of the melody means we, as listeners, can easily grasp its shape and its function. Notice that Josquin begins each section of the melody with slow notes. In this way he makes it easy for us to grasp right away the distinctive features of the melody so that the melodies are much more memorable than the earlier ones by Dufay and Ockeghem. Notice also how short the main "theme" is. There is very little question about how the notes should fit the text, and, in fact, Josquin was highly praised for his sensitivity to text setting in his music, both with regard to his respect of word accents and at the larger level of text expression. The generation following Josquin refined the style of the master. As you can see from melody 6, taken from the motet "Ave regina caelorum" ("Hail, Queen of Heavens") by Nicolas Gombert (d. about 1560), composers of the period 1520 to 1550 liked to work with relatively short motives and to reuse these motives several times in the course of a composition with small variations and changes at each repetition. The excerpt presented here repeats the words "Domina angelorum" ("Lady of the angels"). The two phrases are very similar in their general shape (note, for example, that they both start with the melody going up in similar fashion), but there are also important differences, the most important being where Gombert decides to place rhythmic stress in these lines. For example, the first statement of the words begins with a quarter note on the last beat of a measure, while the second statement begins with a longer note, a half note, on the second beat of a measure. The effect is to shift emphasis throughout the line with small changes of stress on certain notes and syllables. Similar small differences can be observed throughout these two musical phrases, and the overall effect is one of great flexibility in melodic writing. Gombert does not stress too much the "strong" beats of a measure but seems to be trying deliberately to write a melody without strong rhythmic accents. Notice also the almost total absence of leaps in the melodic line and the careful construction of the shape of the melody. The passage begins and ends on F, giving a satisfying sense of arrival at its close. The high point is reached on B-flat in both phrases, stressing the parallelism between the two repetitions, and the first phrase ends on G, a step above the final note. Using the note above the final as an arrival point would have signaled to the Renaissance listener that this is just a temporary resting point: the listener would have then been waiting for a more satisfying return to the final F.

The final example, melody 7, is taken from the works of a composer whose name in the nineteenth century was practically synonymous with Renaissance sacred music: Giovanni Pierluigi da Palestrina (d. 1594). Palestrina's sacred music was long regarded as a model for Catholic sacred music in the late Renaissance, and his influence was such that well over a century after his death, the Viennese theorist J. J. Fux published the treatise *Gradus ad Parnassum* (The Stairway to Parnassus), which was meant to teach Palestrina's style to eighteenth-century composers. The style in which Palestrina wrote his melodies seems to be very similar to Gombert's style, yet there are important differences. One thing you will notice in this excerpt from his sacred motet "Sicut lilium inter spinas" ("Like a Lily among Thorns") is how cleverly Palestrina avoids repeating rhythmic figures. In his music it is very rare to see two consecutive measures with the same rhythmic shape. The first few measures of music unfold elegantly, moving from longer note values to a short flourish in measure 5; in the first eight measures of music we find a rhythmic figure repeated without change only once, when the rhythm (although not the notes) of measure four is repeated in measure six. Toward the end of the passage, as we approach a cadence, Palestrina builds tension and expectation by using a repeated rhythmic figure (dotted quarter note, eighth note, quarter note) in measures seven to nine. Even here only measure eight and nine repeat the rhythmic figure with exactly the same stresses, while measure seven is slightly different. Although Palestrina's melodies often sound almost simple and give the sense of a logical progression, in fact, this apparent simplicity is due to the tremendous care that the composer lavishes on each small detail of the music, with the final effect being that, when we listen to his music, we almost feel that his choices were the only logical ones.

Harmony as Compositional Tool

In the use of harmony as well, we must concentrate on small, more delicate details rather than expect to hear the type of sounds we are accustomed to hear in later repertory. A composer of the time of Beethoven often ends a movement of a symphony with a series of repeated chords and cadences that can signal even to a casual listener that the end has arrived, while a Renaissance composer would use much subtler signals, which might have seemed as forceful to Renaissance listeners as Beethoven's do to us. Cadences in music are points of arrival in a composition where the music arrives at a resting place, free of tension. Cadences are usually employed in the same way we use punctuation in writing. Some cadences, such as the ones customarily found at the end of a classical symphony movement, act like the period at the end of a sentence. Other cadences are more like a semicolon or a comma; they are not supposed to be very forceful but are used to provide a small pause. They can tell the listener that a phrase, a theme, or a motif has reached its end and the composer will soon begin something different.

To an ear unfamiliar with Renaissance music it seems that cadences are encountered much more seldom than in popular music of our era or in the works of Mozart. In reality, composers in the Renaissance had a wider range of possibilities and perhaps used this variety of choices with more subtlety than later composers. Often composers overlapped a cadence with the beginning of the next phrase, avoiding the sense of finality and rest that the cadence brings. In a polyphonic piece it is possible to write a couple of the voices in a way that suggests that a point of arrival is near while, at the same time, the other voices begin a new phrase, thus keeping up the momentum of the piece. In fact, composers in the sixteenth century cultivated the effect of "evading the cadence" (as one theorist called it), that is, of setting up cadences but avoiding their fulfillment. The effect is of a continuous piece of music with little, if any, separation between phrases, moving seamlessly from one section to the next.

On the opposite end of the range we have compositions in which the cadences are not terribly different from those found in modern pop or folk music, that is, very clear-cut and decisive points of rest and arrival. To make a sweeping generalization, we can say that musical genres that were more influenced by popular music and many instrumental genres present a use of cadences that is clear and direct, while much sacred music and the more sophisticated secular music tended to be more subtle in this use. In sum, Renaissance composers, as composers throughout the history of music, knew how to exploit the expectations of their audience regarding musical structure. Composers could use a wide range of technical devices to make the audience feel a point of arrival, to thwart those expectations, or to offer anything in between. The difficulty we have sometimes in hearing some of the subtle signals is due simply to our unfamiliarity with this repertory. Renaissance audiences would have known what the composers were trying to do, and there is no reason why we cannot do the same when we get better acquainted with this music.

TEMPO AND DYNAMICS

We have seen earlier that tempo (the speed of music) and dynamics (the level of loudness) were not usually indicated on Renaissance scores. This does not necessarily mean that composers of the time did not care about these details but only that they allowed some freedom to the performer and that they trusted the performer to know the practices of the time. Renaissance theorists sometimes talk about speed in performance, and even though they are not too precise, it is clear that to them tempo was not entirely up to the performer. In general, a modern performer of Renaissance music will look at a piece and consider its musical features, its intended use (for example, whether it is a secular or a sacred piece), and, if it is a vocal piece, its text. Still it is possible for two modern performers to arrive at tempos that are quite different while performing the same piece. We can take comfort in knowing that Renaissance theorists also could disagree among themselves on the same subject.

Although rudimentary indications of dynamics appear only in a handful of scores from the late Renaissance, we know from accounts of performances that listeners enjoyed hearing different dynamic levels in the same compositions. For example, some singers were praised for the way they used subtle nuances of dynamics to enhance the interpretation of the text they were singing. Other times the composer wrote the music in such a way that the performers were forced to use specific levels of dynamics. Orlando di Lasso, one of the greatest late Renaissance composers, sometimes wrote passages in the lower range of the voices of the choir, forcing them to sing more softly, and then shifted suddenly to high ranges that forced the choir to sing louder, so that, without any other indication in the score, he obtained a particular dynamic contrast.

In general, then, we must be aware that, as far as tempo and dynamics are concerned, almost anything we hear in a modern recording of Renaissance music is the result of the training and the musical sensibility and taste of the performers, rather than being rigidly pre-scribed in the score.

QUESTIONS OF FORM

When we listen to a piece of music, whether we are aware of this or not, we tend to look for patterns and forms. We can recognize rep-etitions of musical phrases or segments where a section of music is meant to contrast with the preceding one. In popular music we en-joy the repetition of a "catchy" tune within a song, and we can easily tell whether two successive melodies are similar or different. The situ-ation is a bit more difficult when we listen to classical music: some-times patterns are easy to spot; other times it takes a trained ear of someone who has had some formal musical studies to recognize, for example, the overall shape of a nineteenth-century symphonic move-ment. Again, we can observe a great amount of variety in Renaissance music in this respect. Much secular music, especially the type that re-lies on more popular models, tends to use simple forms (for example, strophic forms where the several stanzas of text all repeat the same music) just as in most modern pop songs. This is perhaps the easiest form to recognize and one with which we are all familiar.

One example of a clear form in a Renaissance piece can be seen in example 6, which shows a famous tune from the fifteenth century, "L'homme armé" ("The Armed Man"). We can easily tell that the opening section (marked A in the example) is identical to the ending section (also marked A), while the middle section (marked B) provides a contrasting melody. This is what we would normally describe as being an ABA form, thus indicating that the material of the beginning re-turns toward the end. Similar forms (with variants such as AABA, and so forth) are familiar to us because they are still prevalent in modern pop music. Fairly simple forms with much repetition can also be found in Renaissance dance pieces where the dancers needed music that fol-lowed certain established patterns in order to execute the dance steps correctly.

In many Renaissance pieces, though, it is impossible to find simple patterns of repetition, certainly nothing as clear as ABA. When a piece goes from beginning to end without any significant repetition of musical ideas or phrases we call it a "through-composed" piece. This type, which includes a fairly high percentage of Renaissance sacred music, might constitute the most difficult listening for an unprepared

Example 6   Anonymous fifteenth-century chanson, "L'homme armé"

ear. We are conditioned to look for patterns of repetition, the return of a musical phrase or of a refrain, and so on, and when these features are missing, our ears sometimes have trouble making sense of the whole piece. Nevertheless, even in through-composed pieces, it is always possible to listen for details that help give the piece a shape, even without repetitions. For example, a piece might be based on a series of contrasting sections, and often the fact that a contrasting section is beginning is a signal by the composer that something important or noteworthy is happening. As in the case of cadences, sometimes the solutions employed by Renaissance composers require, on the part of the listener, more attention to detail and the willingness to become acquainted with this marvelous repertory.

THE RELATIONSHIP OF TEXT AND MUSIC

Much of the surviving Renaissance music was written for voices and, therefore, is supplied with lyrics, words meant to be set to music. Usually a composer would choose (or be given) a sacred or secular text and would have to write music to set those words. This is fairly common in classical music of all periods. The process employed in modern pop music, where often a musician thinks of a catchy tune before finding words that go with it, was not the normal procedure in the Renaissance. This means that a very important aspect of the work of the composer was deciding how to best adapt the music to the words or, as we call it, the act of text setting. One of the decisions a composer had to make when faced with the challenge of setting a text to music was how to determine the relationship of each individual musical line with the text it had to set. Composers in the Renaissance paid increasing attention to small details of text setting. If, in the fifteenth century, it was not uncommon to see musical accents that contrast with the textual accents or words set with rests between their syllables, in the sixteenth century these "barbarisms" would have been avoided by composers unless a special effect was desired. Beyond that, though, one of the fundamental choices was between a melody in which many notes are sung to a single syllable of text and one in which there is a different note for each syllable. We call the first type of text setting "melismatic," and a passage where that text setting is used is a "melisma." When each syllable receives its own note we call the setting "syllabic." Most pieces will fall somewhere between the two extremes, alternating between syllabic setting and melismatic setting even within one phrase. Certain words and emotions could suggest melismatic writing to a Renaissance composer: expressions of joy and happiness, for example, were often set that way. Syllabic writing was often employed when the text needed to be heard clearly or to imitate a simple "popular" style.

Beyond that, a composer could choose a type of melodic line or a harmony that would enhance the text in various ways. Later sixteenth-century composers often used dissonances when the text spoke of pain or anguish and used consonant harmony when it turned to happiness and love. We can say that by the late sixteenth century a composer was almost like an interpreter of the poetry it set to music. He had to analyze the text to decide which images and concepts were the key ones in the poem, and he had to decide exactly how to convey those feelings to the audience. It is obvious in much Renaissance music that the question of text setting was very important to composers and that they must have spent a great deal of time familiarizing themselves with a given text before setting it to music. The performers acted almost as equal partners in this process and were often praised for their sensitivity and attention to the text. This does not mean that all poems set to music were of equally high quality or serious in nature. There were plenty of lighter poems, often set in the manner of more modern pop songs, in strophic form, that is, with successive stanzas of the poetry repeating the music of the first stanza (a procedure that makes exact attention to the text virtually impossible). On the other hand, we can say that the care taken by composers in setting to music texts of the highest quality represents one of the crowning achievements of the Renaissance.

POPULAR MUSIC AND ART MUSIC

In our modern musical world we draw a fairly distinct line between popular and "art" music. Art (classical) music is performed in concert halls where sedate audiences sit in silence throughout the performance. Performers wear formal attire, many of the audience members seem to be mature adults, and the music is preserved in scores that are studied and followed as closely as possible. Popular music is played in less formal settings; audiences, usually on the young side, cheer and shout, showing their feelings about the performance openly, and performers wear flashy clothes designed to be sexually suggestive or with an anti-establishment message. Most popular music is not learned from scores but is passed on from one musician to the next, if not learned from a CD of a particular performance. Pieces are constantly changed and rearranged by new performers, and improvisation is a considerable part of each performance. Few artists and audience members cross over consistently from one type of music to the other.[3]

If we try to approach Renaissance music by applying our modern concepts of popular and art music, however, we are doomed to a faulty understanding of the musical world of the time. It is important to realize that such a distinction cannot be rigidly applied to Renaissance music without the risk of severe oversimplification of a complex situation. There is no question that we can label some musical genres of the period as more in the "high art" tradition, but often the popular traditions of the time make their presence felt in unexpected ways. In the next section we will explore how these questions apply to the world of Renaissance music.

Written and Unwritten Traditions

Western classical music relies to a great extent on scores to ensure that music will be performed and reach its audience in a way that will respect the intentions of the composer. In our musical tradition this reliance on scores does not apply as strictly to all types of music. Popular, folk, and jazz musicians rely to a greater or lesser extent on an unwritten tradition, that is, on ways of learning pieces of music directly from a teacher or a fellow musician without the need to commit the whole musical text to paper. Conditioned by the reliance of classical musicians on written scores, we tend to think that music that does not rely on scores for its existence and transmission is, almost by definition, inferior in quality and less sophisticated. In fact, many non-Western musical traditions that are primarily passed on orally also manage to be very sophisticated and complex, thus refuting this basic assumption. In Renaissance music we find an example of a Western tradition of art music in which the unwritten oral tradition played a very important role. Even in that most "elitist" of institutions, the church choir, performances were sometimes dependent on improvisation and on unwritten traditions. We know that church singers were trained in providing improvised polyphony so that on occasion a singer would sing a church chant from a book or from memory while another singer improvised another melody to go with it, following very precise rules. Practices such as this confirm that oral, unwritten musical traditions are not limited to simple, popular music but can be extremely sophisticated and not at all inferior to those traditions that rely on scores. Indeed, some unwritten traditions were reserved for the most expert musicians and the most elite audiences and, therefore, should by right have a place in a discussion of art music.

In fact, we can also say that much written music of the Renaissance, even when composed by well-known musicians, seems to include features we normally associate with popular music, such as simple tunes and accompaniment, lyrics that seem down to earth and without sophistication, and simple musical forms. The preceding sentences might seem paradoxical, but the reality is there seems to have been in the Renaissance less of a separation between the popular and the art world, and the dividing line was often crossed in a variety of ways. Musicians might have thought of music as being more a continuum than a series of separate, discrete genres, and this is evidenced by the fact that, for example, composers who are responsible for some of the most sophisticated musical treatments of complex poetry in the sixteenth-century madrigal could also publish collections that imitated, and were influenced by, popular forms.

FOLK MUSIC AND ITS INFLUENCE ON RENAISSANCE MUSIC

The repertory of folk music of the Renaissance did not survive intact. Folk musicians performed without the benefit of musical scores—

in fact some might have been musically illiterate—and, at any rate, most folk traditions are entirely dependent on oral transmission of a repertory, so we don't have for this music scores that we can study. The few glimpses we have of folk traditions of the Renaissance can be found in published compositions that incorporate folk melodies and texts. At various times in the Renaissance, patrons of music seem to have been interested in popular musical expression. In France songs often incorporated tunes and lyrics that would seem inappropriate for the aristocratic circles that cultivated the genre. Similarly, the Habsburg Emperor Maximilian I, one of the greatest music-loving patrons of the Renaissance, encouraged his composers to set German lyrics in simple musical settings, which we call Lieder, or Tenorlieder. In Italy the very sophisticated courts of Mantua and Ferrara were the cradle of the frottola, a genre that arose probably in part as a reaction to the artificiality of much secular music of the fifteenth century. In England manuscripts copied at the court of Henry VIII contain, among other things, simple harmonizations of popular tunes.

It is hard to explain why courts that seem to have been interested in the most sophisticated expression in the visual arts, in architecture, and even in the daily clothes worn at court would so openly imitate popular music, but one explanation might be found in the function of secular music at these courts: pure entertainment meant to amuse and divert the courtiers. There is no question that these repertories have in common a musical and textual immediacy that did not require an effort on the part of the audience comparable to that necessary for other types of music. Often composers would "wink" at the audience by including a popular tune or two in such a way that listeners would recognize the game. The text itself would declare something like "and I started singing . . ." or "and she was singing . . ." or other such signals that what was to follow was going to be a musical quote. An Italian song of the time proclaims: "Now that my mind is dreaming in vain and my steps are wandering, every day I will go singing without shame: 'On the way back from Bologna my shoes are hurting my feet.'" The last sentence is clearly quoting from a popular song. As one can see from this example, the pretext to introduce a well-known tune is often a thin one, and the "borrowed" text might not make perfect sense with the rest of the song. What is important is the playful nature of these pieces.

In conclusion, establishing dividing lines between popular and art music is not as easy in the Renaissance as it might be in our world, where we can assign without any hesitation a Beethoven symphony to the realm of art music and a rap song to popular music. We must also acknowledge that a large quantity of Renaissance art music was passed on orally and probably never committed to paper; thus, entire repertories, for example those of the singers who specialized in improvisation and who were active at Northern Italian courts of the fifteenth century, are for all practical purposes lost to us. We might be able to catch glimpses of this music by examining a few existing pieces that were meant to show amateurs how to move their first steps in this style, but we might never be able to recapture the full impact of music that gives the lie to the concept that only written music is worthy of being called art music.

CONCLUSIONS

In spite of some unfamiliar features, Renaissance music can provide a modern music lover with a rewarding listening experience. The sheer variety of the music of this period allows someone who wishes to approach this repertory to choose those pieces that sound more familiar and easier and gradually gain sufficient familiarity with the music to appreciate the more complex pieces. Most of all, it is important to try and leave behind preconceived notions of musical style that we derive either from the standard classical repertory of today or from pop music. We should also enjoy the freedom that is given to the performers and appreciate the important role (almost a partnership) that a performer has in re-creating this music for a modern audience.

NOTES

1. There are several general books on Renaissance music that could be useful for the interested reader who wishes to find more technical information about the music of the period. The most useful might be Allan W. Atlas, *Renaissance Music* (New York: Norton, 1998) and Leeman Perkins, *Music in the Age of the Renaissance* (New York: Norton, 1999).

2. Quoted in Glenn Watkins, *Gesualdo: The Man and His Music*, 2nd ed. (Oxford: Clarendon Press, 1991), 68.

3. An engaging discussion of music in popular culture and of popular traditions in general can be found in Peter Burke, *Popular Culture in Early Modern Europe*, rev. reprint (Aldershot: Ashgate, 1994).

CHAPTER 2

The Life of a Renaissance Musician

RENAISSANCE MUSICIANS: PROFESSIONALS AND AMATEURS

Many Renaissance artists were considered by their contemporaries only as very gifted craftsmen. For example, even famous and important painters like Titian painted subjects commissioned to them by wealthy patrons instead of fulfilling their artistic vision, although the artists' individuality could flourish very well even within these limitations. Furthermore, virtually every painter and visual artist availed himself of the help of apprentices and aides who often completed substantial sections of a work of art. Although this process was perfectly acceptable to Renaissance patrons, to us this seems like an unacceptable breach of artistic code, which demands that every painting be the expression of the innermost drive and artistry of a single artist.

In music, performers were usually considered to be employees subject to the demands of their employers and required to perform what and when their patrons asked. That is not to say that Renaissance employers did not appreciate various levels of artistry but simply that they assumed that their social inferiors (the musicians) would obey them according to the social rules of the period. The situation was slightly different for composers. Up until the sixteenth century, many of the most important composers were not what we might call professional musicians. Composers such as Philippe de Vitry (1291–1361) and Guillaume de Machaut (ca. 1300–1377) in the fourteenth century and John Dunstable (d. 1453) in the early fifteenth century were first and foremost high court or church officials, charged with important affairs of state, diplomatic correspondence, and other tasks of this nature. Dunstable, hailed by the theorist Johannes Tinctoris as the "fount and origin" of the new "sweet" style of fifteenth-century music, was known as a mathematician and astronomer, and it is clear that, important as it might seem to the music historian, his music occupied only a relatively small part of his life. Furthermore, Dunstable was the social equal of other courtiers, and even his noble patrons might not have been able to order him to compose. If the ruler at the court employing Dunstable (let us not forget, as court official, not composer) wanted to hear a new composition by him, he would have to couch such a request in flowery and diplomatic language, for example, by expressing his desire to hear one of his inimitable compositions, in other words, ask for a "favor" rather than make a demand on a subordinate. The fact that the subordinate could hardly refuse such a polite request without offending the patron does not mean that his position was similar to that of a servant.

In the sixteenth century, on the other hand, composers became more professionalized. The first instance of a musician receiving an important appointment solely for his compositional skills is that of the Flemish Heinrich Isaac, hired by the Emperor Maximilian I as Hofkomponist ("court composer") in 1497. Apparently Isaac was not required to attend court regularly and was not charged with the usual tasks of the director of music of a court, such as training the choirboys or conducting the choir. Most sixteenth-century composers continued to be expected to lead choirs or attend to a musical establishment, but the most important change is that now these musicians made a living almost entirely from their musical skills, although they sometimes sought other ways to increase their income. Paradoxically, the increasing professionalization of composers also made them more like the employees that performers already were, because the process made the distinction between the aristocratic amateur and the professional composer a sharper one. By the late sixteenth century, aristocrats or high court officials were supposed to be well versed in music and perhaps to be able to compose but without showing off these gifts. To make a show of one's musical abilities, on the other hand, was considered improper and a cause for somewhat negative comments from others.

When Prince Carlo Gesualdo of Venosa (d. 1613), one of the most interesting and unconventional composers of the late sixteenth century, met other aristocrats, he would mystify them by his dedication to music, a self-centered and almost manic interest in an activity that, according to the aristocratic code of behavior of the times, was supposed to be only a pastime. When Gesualdo traveled to the northern Italian city of Ferrara in 1594 to marry the cousin of the Duke Alfonso II, the courtier escorting him on this trip sent letters ahead, as was customary in these cases, describing the prince in detail. The courtier, Alfonso Fontanelli, writes of course in very diplomatic language, but it is obvious that he considers some of Gesualdo's behavior to be strange. In one of his letters he says that Gesualdo wanted to talk only about hunting and music, declaring himself an authority on both (this boasting being already a breach of the aristocratic code of conduct). "On hunting," says Fontanelli, "he did not enlarge very much, since he did not find much reaction from me, but about music he spoke at such length that I have not heard so much in a whole year. He makes open profession of it [music] and shows his works in score to everybody in order to induce them to marvel at his art."[1] Even from this cautious language we can sense the disapproval of Fontanelli, who, later in his letter, also diplomatically refuses to give his opinion about the music composed by the prince, who played the lute for him for an hour and a half. Gesualdo was breaking the aristocratic code by not treating his pastimes with sufficient nonchalance and by insisting that a guest such as Fontanelli look at his music and comment on it. The correct behavior would have been to wait for Fontanelli to beg the prince to show him his music and, after many demurrals, to show the music, all the while insisting that the pieces were just trifles and unworthy of serious considerations, and so on. When Fontanelli writes that the prince makes "open profession" of music, he is in fact almost insulting, accusing the prince of acting like a paid musician.

A sense of the usual social distance between employers and musicians and of the expectations placed on musicians can be acquired by reading contemporary documents and letters. In a famous letter written in 1570, the composer Giovanni Pierluigi da Palestrina, by then one of the most respected musicians of his time, responds to a request by Duke Vincenzo Gonzaga of Mantua in a way that shows him to be fully aware of the social distance between them. Duke Vincenzo, who was an amateur composer, had sent Palestrina some of his own compositions to be judged by the master. Palestrina responds in typically flowery language:

> I say that just as your Excellency surpasses nature in all your works, so in Music you exceed those who worthily make it their profession; and the better to contemplate it, I have parted [i.e., scored] the Motet, and

having seen the fair, uncommon artistry, and how the words are given a living spirit, in accordance with the meaning, I have marked some places, for it seems to me that if one could do without them, the Harmony would sound better.

And after some further criticism of the ducal compositions, he says: "It is evident that your Excellency knows these trifles better than I do, but I have said this in order to obey you, and so shall I obey you whenever you will favor me by commanding [your] affectionate and most obliged servant."[2] What is evident to us is that Palestrina is trying as hard as possible to be diplomatic about the shortcomings of the piece sent to him by Duke Vincenzo. A more blunt criticism, such as the one that Palestrina might have given to a pupil, would have been unthinkable toward a patron as powerful as the duke, and Palestrina had to tread lightly or risk alienating someone with widespread connections among patrons of music.

If this was the social gap between one of the masters of the sixteenth century and a powerful aristocrat, we can easily imagine the size of the gap between the same aristocrat and the average musician. There were exceptions, of course, and none were more glaring than that of the Flemish composer Orlando di Lasso, who served with distinction at the court of Munich in Germany from 1556 to his death in 1594. Lasso, who is described in some letters as "a great buddy" with a fun disposition, became very close to Wilhelm, the heir to the ducal throne in Munich and who was approximately his age, primarily through their common interests in music, dancing, and even acting. For example, Lasso played an important part in the festivities surrounding the wedding of Wilhelm in 1568, acting in an Italian comedy staged for the occasion. As a result, Lasso's relationship with his employer, when the heir became Duke Wilhelm V, can only be described as unusual if not downright unique. We have many letters written by Lasso, who was often traveling, to Duke Wilhelm, and in them the composer, using a humorous mixture of French, Spanish, Italian, German, and Latin, dares to write sentences that would have doomed a regular employee of the court. Even though it is impossible to convey the full flavor of these letters in translation, here is a passage from a letter written in 1572. Even in the opening address, Lasso mocks the overly flowery opening of many similar letters: "Most High, Most Mighty, and Flighty Lord, my master forevermore." Most of the letter is almost in verse form, and Lasso writes breezily of his travels. At the close he goes even further: "My wife, my little Rudolf, and Mr. my own person do kiss in all humility the hands of Your Excellency and of our madam the Princess, while her rump feels no distress. God preserve our cheerfulness."[3] For almost anyone else, such a remark about the wife of the ruler would have been unthinkable, but apparently Wilhelm treated Lasso almost like a brother, erasing the considerable social difference between the two. While cases such as Lasso's, although rare, did exist, we must remember that musicians were seen normally as employees of a church or a court and treated accordingly.

Renaissance society followed the ideals of the Greek philosophers Plato and Aristotle, who considered professional musicians inferior to the "gentleman." Aristotle put it in very strong terms in his *Politics*: "We may accordingly reject any professional system of instruction [in music]. By that we mean any system intended to prepare pupils for competition. . . . That is why we regard [this type of] performance as something improper in a freeman, and more befitting a hireling. The standards by which they fix their aim [i.e., the pleasure of their audience] is a bad standard: the commonness of the audience tends to debase the quality of the music."[4] Although Renaissance attitudes toward music were less extreme, the statement of one of the most influential classical thinkers still affected the views of the "gentlemen" of the time. Writing in his *Book of the Courtier*, easily the best-known book on aristocratic manners in the sixteenth century, the Italian courtier Baldessare Castiglione (himself described by contemporaries as the epitome of the gentleman) made clear that in the field of music the perfect gentleman of the court (the courtier) ought to behave in such a way as to exclude the possibility of being confused with a professional musician. He writes:

> I would not our Courtier should do as many do, that as soon as they come to any place, and also in the presence of great men with whom they have no acquaintance at all, without much entreating set out themselves to show as much as they know—yea and many times they know not—so that a man would think they came purposely to show themselves for that, and that is their principal profession. Therefore, let our Courtier come to show his music as a thing to pass the time, and as he were enforced to do it, and not in the presence of noble men, nor of any great multitude . . . and let him make semblant that he esteemeth but little in himself that quality, but in doing excellently well make it much esteemed of other men.[5]

Thus, ideally the amateur gentleman had to achieve a very high level of proficiency while showing to the rest of the world that he still valued the teaching of the ancient Greek philosophers. The word "amateur," which for us has acquired a somewhat pejorative tone, did not necessarily mean a lowering of musical standards but was often simply the result of strict social limits placed on the practice of music. It is true that a few members of the lower nobility, especially in the late sixteenth and early seventeenth century, did end up pursuing musical careers, but they often kept up appearances by being listed in the payrolls as "gentlemen of the court" rather than musicians. We have hints that this sometimes created problems for the noblemen in question. Giulio Cesare Brancaccio, a minor aristocrat who also sang bass for the Duke of Ferrara's "chamber" singers, often balked at being summoned for a performance in the duke's private apartments because he felt such summons put him on the same level as a professional musician. Eventually, the duke grew tired of his attitude and dismissed him from the court.

In general, though, the distinction between the full-time professional musician and the "amateur" is fairly easy to establish. The picture would not be complete, however, without noting that there were many musicians who did not fall into either category. In every Renaissance city there would be many people with nonmusical jobs who also occasionally performed professionally. It is not unusual to see in a legal document someone described with expressions such as "boatman and lute player" or "clerk and instrumentalist." Priests, who always received some musical training, could be employed as singers on special occasions to increase the size of a choir. Lower class instrumentalists played for festivals and private celebrations, as well as in public dance halls. Of course these part-time musicians are harder to trace in documents of the period, but what we have as far as evidence is sufficient to suggest that the space between the full-time professional and the "pure" amateur was populated by a variety of musicians.

THE LIFE OF A SINGER: CHURCH AND COURT

Even within the world of professional musicians there were obvious divisions and a definite hierarchy. If we can identify the elite of Renaissance musicians, it would consist principally of the singers and composers of sacred music, those whose primary function was performance for the most important churches of the time, where religion often mixed freely with politics. Admission to this group was not easy and was strictly prohibited to women. The musician went through a

Sodoma, *St. Benedict excommunicates two believers* (detail). In typical Renaissance fashion, a small choir of church singers crowds around a single book of music on a music stand. (Courtesy of Scala, Art Resource, New York.)

rigorous period of apprenticeship and study, usually beginning as a young boy, when he was identified as someone with musical gifts. At church schools, boys were trained to become priests and were instructed in many subjects, including the singing of Gregorian chant, which was expected of every priest. Those with some aptitude for singing would then be instructed in the singing of polyphonic music, and the better boys would soon start singing with the church choir. In an era when women were not allowed to sing in church (except in cloistered convent churches), boys and adults singing in falsetto provided the voices for the upper parts of the choir. Most of these boys, especially in northern European cathedral schools of the fifteenth century, would be also trained in musical composition. When the boys reached puberty and their voices broke, they could rejoin the choir if their adult singing voice was deemed of sufficient quality, or they could continue their education and be ordained as priests. In either case, the son of a lower middle-class family could look forward to a long and honorable career within the confines of the church.

Beginning in the fifteenth century, in a period of expansion of the practice of polyphonic singing in church, we notice that southern European church choirs, especially those in Italy, began to compete for northern-trained singers, recruiting them with increased salaries and perks, and trying to lure them away from competing choirs. It is obvious that as the singing of elaborate music in church became more common, church officials and secular rulers began to see music as one of the ways to display their religious piety and devotion. In the same way that they spent on paintings, statues, mosaics, new churches and side chapels, vestments, and other elements necessary for the divine service, they felt that having a very good choir would reflect favorably on themselves as rulers and on the entire state. An example of this attitude is found in a decree of the governors of the ducal chapel of St. Mark's in Venice, dating from the year 1403, that established a singing school for eight local boys at the church. The rationale for the establishment of the school is given as follows: "Since it is to the honor and fame of our state that there be good singers in our church of Saint Mark's, because said church is the foremost church of our city, we have decided . . . to hire eight choirboys, native of our city, who must learn to sing well."[6] The language used ("to the honor and fame of our state") is similar to that found in other documents dealing with the decoration of the church or the regulations meant to ensure that ceremonies were celebrated with the solemnity appropriate for the importance of the Venetian republic. This suggests that, by this time, music was seen as an equally important adornment of church ceremonies in Venice.

While church singers usually would not be paid enough to become wealthy, their life could be very comfortable and also provide them with respect and a solid social status. In addition, since many of them were ordained clergy, they could benefit from appointments to clerical positions both near and far. Some were the so-called "sinecures" (from the Latin "sine cura," meaning "without a burden"), ecclesiastical appointments given solely for the purposes of increasing the income of the singer but without the expectation that the individual would actually be required to be present and fulfill the obligations of the job. Up to the time of the Protestant Reformation sinecures were important sources of income for musicians, but the Council of Trent (1545–1563), the gathering that began the Catholic Counter-Reformation, limited severely the use of these benefices.

Although we have a sizable quantity of documents from churches of the period, reconstructing the life of a musician is not necessarily made easier by the kind of official documents that have survived. From those we usually learn information such as the size of a particular choir, the voice distribution, the names of the singers and their region or city of provenance, their salary, their disciplinary problems or instances of exceptional service, and so on. Reading these documents literally, though, can lead to some misunderstanding. For example, we would assume, given the example of our professional musical organizations, that the existence of a choir of twenty singers at a church would mean the presence of all the singers not otherwise sick or unable to attend at every religious service. In practice, most, if not all, singers of a church would have other duties, and regular services might not include elaborate singing or include only a small quantity of it. The full choir would be in attendance for important occasions, as required by the bishop or local secular ruler, but often at other services many singers would be singing elsewhere as freelancers, performing religious services in other churches, tending to their business affairs, staying home because of sickness, or being away on extended leaves of absence whether approved by their employers or not. Understanding employers would often turn a blind eye to the practice, because closing off these sources of income might have created more demands for higher salaries, which they were not prepared to offer. Occasionally, church singers could have occupations or businesses outside the church. Giovanni Pierluigi da Palestrina, who spent almost his whole life in the service of various church choirs, took as his second wife the well-to-do widow of a Roman fur merchant and spent the last years of his life managing her business and finances with a great degree of success (thus making a lie of the popularly held notion that great artists are clueless on practical everyday matters).

A typical day for the singers of the chapel would depend on what the religious calendar had in store. On a ferial day (any day when no important feast was celebrated) most singers might be free to do as they pleased for most of the day. Some members of the choir trained younger singers or choirboys; others took lessons themselves from the director, rehearsed music, or often sought to find occasional employment at private functions or local celebrations in other churches or monasteries of the city. Some would spend their time composing new music or copying music for the use of the choir. It was on the feast days that singers would be most busy. A major feast day in a Catholic church would begin with the celebration of the Vespers service, a traditional prayer service centered around the reading or singing of Psalms, on the evening of the preceding day and continue through the Vespers of the feast day, with at least a high Mass on that day. Often, especially on occasions that mixed religion and politics, there would be processions meant, at least in part, to impress the populace with the tangible symbols of power and piety. For these celebrations, much polyphony would be sung. On major feast days not only all regular singers would be required to attend, but often additional singers or instrumentalists would be hired to give an even more splendid musical performance as part of the liturgy. Important feast days, such as Easter or the day of the patron saint of a city, meant a time of great demand for competent musicians. We hear a constant stream of complaints from church authorities that musicians salaried by a particular church would feign illness or use other excuses to avoid singing on feast days at the church from which they drew their regular salaries. Although the ones found cheating were usually penalized by their institutions, this was not a great deterrent, since often they could more than make up for the fine by contracting their services out to the highest bidder. Some churches resorted to an elaborate system of fines to be deducted from a singer's salary. The Sistine Chapel (the chapel of the pope) set up a graduated system of fines, depending on the lateness of the singer for a particular service.

In addition, when not on duty at the church, singers and musicians did not always behave in a manner appropriate to their status. The transgressions by those who were members of the clergy seem more shocking to us, but we must remember that until relatively late in the sixteenth century, a priest who served as a singer might have been a priest in name only and very uninterested in matters of the church. As late as the eighteenth century there is the example of the great Venetian composer Antonio Vivaldi, an ordained priest (he was nicknamed "the red priest" because of his red hair), who was very rarely involved in performing priestly duties. When asked by church authorities about his failure to say Mass, Vivaldi often invoked poor health as an excuse, but this poor health did not prevent him from traveling, performing, acting as an impresario for opera, and teaching.

Whether this was deserved or not, the public often saw musicians (both laymen and members of the clergy) as fun loving and unruly, prone to drinking, gambling, and womanizing. At any rate, until the middle of the sixteenth century it was not unusual for priests to live more or less openly with women and to acknowledge somewhat openly the existence of children from these relationships. A typical case is that of a singer, Francesco, nicknamed Zeffiro (Zephyr), who in his will left all of his possessions to his housekeeper and to her daughter, who had been born in his house, a young girl suspiciously named Zeffirina, "no matter whose daughter she might be." These examples of unacceptable behavior were severely curtailed by the new regulations imposed by the Council of Trent, and a major effort was undertaken in Catholic countries to give a better training to priests and to hold them to higher ethical standards.

Good singers could also expect to travel extensively in pursuit of increasingly better jobs. In the fifteenth and sixteenth centuries the major choirs were composed of singers from a wide geographical area, covering most of Western Europe. French, Flemish, and Netherlander singers were most in demand in this period, and it was not infrequent for a singer to change employment frequently, sometimes because of political upheaval but often simply because the competition among courts and churches was extremely fierce, and they were recruited by competing institutions. Court singers also traveled as part of diplomatic missions or military campaigns involving their employer, giving them the chance to meet other musicians and possibly to exchange important musical information. John Dunstable, for example, served the Duke of Bedford, the English regent on the French mainland during the last part of the Hundred Years' War, and it is likely that his service there was an important reason why Dunstable's new musical style became known and appreciated on the Continent. Guillaume

Dufay traveled in Italy in the 1430s when he served the pope as singer of his choir. A stay in Florence on the occasion of the consecration of the cathedral there in 1436, an event attended by the pope, enabled him to begin a friendship with the Medici family, the most important family of international bankers of the fifteenth century, a connection that continued all of his life.

Naturally, there were also many church singers who survived by singing in minor churches, badly paid and often in dire financial straits, far from the glamour of the best churches and courts; in fact, they might have been the majority, but it is indisputable that the best church singers were able to pursue a career full of all kinds of rewards.

Another career available for singers was to be hired primarily to provide chamber music at a court. There was, of course, some overlap, in that singers hired for the needs of a cathedral choir might also perform at court, or court musicians might be asked to perform and compose sacred music, but in many court payrolls we find distinctions between the choir for the church and the singers of secular music. The singer of chamber music at court was expected to provide entertainment for the court or for the inner circle of the ruler. Sometimes these singers could be presented at banquets and festivities staged for visiting royalty or aristocrats, although we would not call these performances public. Other times they would perform in the private apartments of the ruler for only a few lucky souls. There is evidence that on occasion the employers had a proprietary feeling toward these musicians and their music. When composers in their employ wrote new songs, patrons might consider these to have become, in effect, their property and that they could control the way these pieces were allowed to circulate outside the court, if they were allowed to circulate at all. The competition among courts was such that patrons wanted to be able to impress their guests with music they had never heard before, and the only way to ensure that was to control the music written by one's musicians. As a result, employment at court depended partly on musical fashion and trends. In the fifteenth century, when the dominating secular genre was the French chanson, some Italian courts imported French singers and composers in order to have the most fashionable music.

Other courts cultivated the figure of the improviser, the poet-composer who improvised poetry, music, or both, obviously by using well-worn patterns committed to memory. Some of these singers were among the highest paid musicians at court and were the subject of effusive praise. At the death of one of the most famous, Serafino Ciminelli, known as Aquilano, a volume was prepared that included a short biography and the contributions of his many admirers. Although, as many other improvisers, he left no written musical compositions, we have some information about his style in the biography, which concludes with this assessment: "In reciting his poems he was so passionate and matched the music with the words so judiciously that he moved equally the souls of his listeners, whether wise or mediocre or plebeian or female. His death was widely lamented by contemporary poets, who thereby saw our age stripped of no small ornament."[7]

Not every court singer reached this pinnacle of success and, in actuality, life at court could be difficult, dependent as it was on the mood and the preferences of the ruler. Even Serafino, in fact, is described in his biography as being at odds with one of his employers, the Cardinal Ascanio Sforza, who—writes the biographer—"(like most princes, and not unjustly) wanted Serafino to conform to his own ways," causing "anger and annoyance"[8] in the artist.

INSTRUMENTALISTS

The situation of Renaissance instrumentalists was somewhat different. Without the limitations imposed by the clerical status, instrumentalists often passed their trade from father to son in musical families that extended for generations. These professional family ties were, of course, the norm in many other professions in the Middle Ages and the Renaissance. The children of a craftsman were expected and encouraged to follow in the footsteps of their father, and this system— as limiting as it might seem to us—had obvious advantages. First of all, it made it possible to pass on the "tricks of the trade" within the family, and it allowed a son, and sometimes a daughter, to take over the father's business, thus avoiding unnecessary expenses and start-up costs. A typical case is that of the goldsmith and artist Benvenuto Cellini, one of the most flamboyant figures of the Renaissance. He tells us in his entertaining, though somewhat unreliable, autobiography that his grandfather had been an architect and his father, Giovanni, had also started along the path. Giovanni also taught himself drawing and music because he believed, as did almost everybody in the Renaissance, that some knowledge of music was necessary for an architect in order to understand proportions and to produce elegant architecture. Giovanni, however, "fell in love with music, which became a second wife for him, and, perhaps because of that little flute which he played far too much, the fifers of the Signory [i.e., the official instrumental band of town pipers hired by the government of Florence] asked him to join them. For a time he played with them merely to amuse himself, and then they pestered him into becoming a member of their band." Giovanni at this point had left his original career, the profession of his father, and was embarking on a new course. But what happened later shows that leaving one's chosen profession was not always so easy. Here is how Benvenuto Cellini continues the story: "Later on, when Lorenzo de' Medici and his son Piero [the rulers of Florence], who were very fond of him, saw that he was spending all his time on the fife, and so *neglecting his real talents and his fine profession*, they had him removed from the band. My father took this very badly, convinced that they had wronged him deeply."[9] Showing a penchant for defying authority, Benvenuto decided to follow in his father's and grandfather's footsteps, even though his own father wanted him to become a musician!

A musician coming from a professional family could be an accomplished performer at a very early age, while still an adolescent, primarily because of the caliber of instruction he could get within his own family. That we have virtually no manuals intended for the training of professional instrumentalists is also a result of this system, where individual instruction from a family member did not depend on the use of textbooks. Often the Renaissance instructional manuals that survive are geared toward amateurs and give us only glimpses of the skills expected of a professional. Once the young musician was admitted to playing with the other instrumentalists, his job would often be regulated by a guildlike organization. In many cities' unions or guilds, of instrumentalists voted on the admission of new members, punished members who had broken the rules, established minimum fees for certain types of services, tried to restrain competition among musicians (which would have brought down everyone's income), and took care of sick and disabled members and, after their death, of their widows and children. In short, much more often than church singers—a notoriously fractious lot—instrumentalists behaved just like the members of any other medieval or Renaissance guild for any of the numerous professions.

Instrumentalists employed at courts were not normally members of guilds, at least as far as their court service was concerned. Some of them, especially lutenists and keyboard players, were often in a very privileged position. The court keyboard player served quite often as a church organist in addition to providing solo performances and accompanying singers and instrumentalists. In Renaissance thought, keyboard instruments and lutes were considered most appropriate for court entertainments and were also among the instruments that a gentleman or a lady could play without overstepping the boundaries of propriety.

Wind bands were also common groups, found in virtually every European city. Almost every ruler employed a wind band to play not only for the court's entertainment but also at civic and religious processions. This band accompanied the ruler as one of the visible symbols of power, and its members benefited from their association with their important duties. Life at court was, of course, much less free than for the instrumentalists who formed guilds in the city. The ruler had an almost unlimited power to hire, fire, raise one's salary, and give gifts and other forms of compensation, and his (or, more rarely, her) will was also the final authority on all court matters. With some exceptions, the majority of instrumentalists would be paid slightly less than singers and composers, and the quality of life at court hinged on the personality of the ruler and could change at a moment's notice when the scepter of command passed hands. Often, if a music-loving ruler was succeeded by someone less interested in music (or more fiscally responsible), several musicians would have to find a new job in a hurry. A sovereign interested in music would spare no expense to secure the best musicians, to buy music books or have them copied, or to purchase the best musical instruments available. Such a sovereign also displayed proudly the musical ensemble that cost so much effort and so much money. The Hapsburg Emperor Maximilian I (1459–1519) commissioned a series of prints known as "The Triumph of Maximilian I," depicting his court entourage. In this grandiose work, music is given a very important place, with several of the prints showing in great detail the various musical groups serving the emperor. Similarly, the music-loving Archduke of Bavaria commissioned a series of lavishly illustrated music manuscripts (at a time, incidentally, when the copying of such manuscripts was on the wane), showing in their illustrations some impressive portraits of the combined musical forces available at court. In almost all these types of illustrations, the choir that sang church music (sometimes accompanied by its own instrumentalists) is shown separately from the other musical groups of instrumentalists, showing that the divisions between these groups was still keenly felt at the time. Rulers would spare almost no effort to secure musicians worthy of their court. Henry VIII, who was an avid amateur musician and a dancer (passing these qualities on to his daughter Elizabeth I), spent a large sum of money on music. As a reward for his expenses, Henry had a group of instrumentalists at his court that could rival that of any other European court of the time.

The life of an instrumentalist could also be split between playing and other activities. In addition to playing, a number of instrumentalists were also involved with the instrument-making business. One of the most interesting and famous examples in the sixteenth century is that of the Bassano family. We first find the Bassanos in Venice in the early part of the century, active as instrumentalists and instrument makers, recent immigrants from the small town of Bassano on the Venetian mainland. Within a generation, some of the family members had been hired by the English king Henry VIII as court instrumentalists, while others remained in Venice. The contacts between the two branches of the family continued for quite a while, and the Bassanos became famous all over

Hans Burgkmair, from *The Triumph of Maximilian I*, "The fifers of the Emperor." This woodcut shows players of shawms and rauschpfeife, both loud double-reed instruments, although it might look like they are playing some kind of trumpet. An instrument case hangs from each saddle, so that the instruments can be put away safely while riding. (Courtesy of Dover.)

Europe, not only as players but also because of the quality of the instruments they manufactured.[10] This was not an isolated case, and we have examples of families of lute makers, for example the German Tieffenbruckers, spanning several countries and generations, keeping contacts and perhaps business dealings among the various branches of the family. The increase in the demand for musical instruments that made all this possible goes hand in hand with the increase in demand for music in the sixteenth century, as musical literacy became a desirable attribute in well-educated ladies and gentlemen.

Families of instrument makers tended to behave like the families of professional instrumentalists, in that such families had a fairly high incidence of intermarriage, with the daughter of the owner of a shop often marrying either one of the workers or the son of another instrument maker. In some cases, marrying the boss's daughter was seen as a condition to be able to take over the business. From the father's standpoint such an arrangement meant he did not have to supply any further dowry for his daughter or to spend the money necessary to have her join a convent. The continuity in his business gained by such an arrangement also insured him against the vagaries of old age, allowing his daughter and son-in-law to care for him while advancing the family business.

Teaching was also an important source of income for musicians, even as it is now. We know very little about these arrangements because they were usually between private parties and rarely involved the drawing up of legal documents or payment notices. We do know that musicians sometimes described themselves as music teachers, but we can only guess at the extent of their activities. An important part of professional musical training was, of course, taken up by church schools. The musical education of the children of the upper nobility was entrusted to court musicians, and there was a lack of organized music schools or conservatories of the type common in our modern world, thus the possibilities for employment as teacher must have been somewhat limited. We know, however, that members of the nobility and of the higher middle-class hired musicians to give music and dancing lessons for their children, although we do not know as much as we would like about the methods employed or the contents of these lessons.

WOMEN MUSICIANS

Another important change occurring during the Renaissance is the beginning of the employment of women as "professional" musicians in the late sixteenth century. Up until the last quarter of the century, women's access to the musical profession was severely limited. Cut off from the main avenues for professional training and performance (the churches and the instrumental guilds), women usually from the nobility or the wealthy bourgeoisie practiced music only as amateurs. Isabella d'Este, the wife of the Marquis of Mantua, was born into the ruling family of the duchy of Ferrara, enjoying the privileges of rank and wealth. She received musical training from the court composer Johannes Martini and was praised as a singer and player on the lute and harpsichord (although she is said to have remarked that she knew such praises were not entirely truthful). Similarly, Queen Elizabeth I, daughter of Henry VIII of England, was taught music and dancing as a young girl, remaining an avid music lover all of her life. She often arranged to be "surprised" by an important ambassador or nobleman while she played the virginal (a small harpsichord). As a queen, she could not give a performance in front of her inferiors, but the elaborate arrangement saved her dignity while giving her a chance to show off her skills and reap praises. Queen Isabella of Spain (1451–1504), the sponsor of Christopher Columbus's discovery voyages, was so interested in music in her chapel that she made sure performances there reached certain standards. One of her chroniclers wrote:

> If anyone of those who were saying or singing the psalms, or other things of the church, made any slip in diction or in the placing of a syllable, she heard and noted it, and afterwards—as teacher to pupil—she emended and corrected it for them.[11]

The practice of music among women of the nobility was sanctioned by the manual of courtly behavior, *The Book of the Courtier*, which described the perfect lady of the court.

> And therefore in dancing I would not see her use too swift and violent tricks, nor yet in singing and playing upon instruments those hard and fast divisions [i.e., musical passages] that declare more cunning than sweetness. Likewise the instruments of music which she useth, in mine opinion, ought to be fit for this purpose. Imagine with yourself what an unsightly matter it were to see a woman play upon a tambour or drum, or blow in a flute or trumpet, or any like instrument; and this because the boisterousness of them doth cover and take away that sweet mildness which setteth so forth every deed that a woman doeth. Therefore when she cometh to dance, or to show any kind of music, she ought to be brought to it with suffering herself somewhat to be prayed, and

with a certain bashfulness that may declare the noble shyness that is contrary to headiness.[12]

From this passage we can see the kind of obstacles that the code of behavior among the upper classes posed to women. Any display of virtuosity or any open desire to perform, in short those qualities so obvious among the best performers, would be seen as entirely inappropriate and would be considered a negative element. In some cases even this limited involvement in music was not allowed to women. The scholar Pietro Bembo, himself a great lover of music, responded quite negatively when his daughter Elena requested permission to learn to play a keyboard instrument:

> I will explain to you something you are perhaps too young to know: playing music is for a woman a vain and frivolous thing. And I would wish you to be the most serious and chaste woman alive. Therefore set aside thoughts of this frivolity and work to be humble and good and wise and obedient. Content yourself with writing and cooking: if you do these two pursuits well you will have accomplished much.[13]

There were, of course, situations when women performers did not seem out of place.

Women could perform sacred music when the performers were nuns. We know that their singing, often predictably described as angelic, attracted visitors to convent churches. At the other end of the spectrum, the only female musicians to approximate a professional status were courtesans and actresses. Courtesans were expected to entertain their clients in a way that was rather different from that of the common prostitute. They were usually educated, even learned, and were able to conduct a conversation on a variety of topics, to write poetry, to sing, and to play. Some were extremely accomplished. The Venetian courtesan Veronica Franco, for example, is considered an important poet of the sixteenth century. She was so famous that when the French king Henry III traveled to Venice for an official visit in 1574, one of his requests was to spend an evening with her, a request the Venetian government happily granted. When an Italian courtesan died in 1514, a diarist reported that "she sang in an excellent way, and she was very famous among musicians, and at her house all kinds of [musical] virtues gathered. And in eight days the musicians of the city will have a solemn Mass said for her at the church of Saint Catherine, and other religious services for her soul."[14] In fact, courtesans often moved in virtually the same circles as wealthy middle-class or noble women, and it is interesting that often the praises of the musical ability of a noncourtesan are accompanied by a great deal of pointed remarks about her virtues and honesty, so she would not be confused with a "professional."

In the later part of the century another type of female musician began to appear. Beginning in selected northern Italian courts, female singers of incredible technical and interpretive skills were engaged to sing a new type of highly difficult secular music for the private enjoyment of a small circle of the court elite. Initially, their status was often disguised, and they were described in court records as "ladies-in-waiting," but it soon became obvious that the only real service they provided was to be ready for musical performances. These women also sang in the increasingly elaborate court productions that included scenery and pageantry, the so-called "intermedi," often appearing in elaborate costumes and with the accompaniment of special effects. The complete professionalization of women musicians, however, did not really take place until opera became established in the seventeenth century, offering women an opportunity for international fame on the stage and placing the most successful of them among the highest paid musicians of the time. In spite of their musical success, women singers were not free of the societal limitations faced by all women of the period. Often their career was managed and directed by the men in their lives—husbands, fathers, patrons—who stood to benefit from the financial success of their charges. Some might have suffered also from the association of music with courtesans, which meant that patrons might have seen women professional musicians as fair game for sexual advances. Nevertheless, in spite of these obstacles, a new area of expression was opened to women that would have been unthinkable only a few decades earlier.

NOTES

1. Quoted and translated in Glenn Watkins, *Gesualdo: The Man and His Music,* 2d ed. (Oxford: Clarendon Press, 1991), 45.

2. The two passages quoted can be found in Piero Weiss, ed. *Letters of Composers Through Six Centuries* (Philadelphia: Chilton, 1967), 16–17.

3. Weiss, *Letters of Composers,* 17.

4. Aristotle, *The Politics,* transl. with an introduction, notes and appendixes by Ernest Barker (Oxford: Clarendon Press, 1946), 348.

5. Baldassare Castiglione, *The Book of the Courtier,* transl. by Thomas Hoby (S.l.: The National Alumni, 1907), 106–7.

6. The original of this document is found in the Archivio di Stato di Venezia (Venetian State Archive), in the records of the Collegio (a government body) for 17 June 1403.

7. Quoted and translated in *The Renaissance*, ed. by Gary Tomlinson, in *Source Readings in Music History*, Oliver Strunk, ed., vol. 3, rev. ed. (New York: W. W. Norton, 1998), 47.

8. Tomlinson, *The Renaissance*, 44.

9. The passages are taken from: Benvenuto Cellini, *The Autobiography*, transl. and with an introduction by George Bull (Harmondsworth, Middlesex: Penguin Books, 1956), 20–21.

10. On the Bassanos, see David Lasocki, with Roger Prior, *The Bassanos: Venetian Musicians and Instrument Makers in England, 1531–1665* (Aldershot: Scolar Press, 1995).

11. Quoted and translated in Tess Knighton, "The Spanish Court of Ferdinand and Isabella," in *The Renaissance*, ed., Iain Fenlon (Englewood Cliffs, NJ: Prentice Hall, 1989), 343.

12. Castiglione, *The Courtier*, 203.

13. Quoted and translated in Tomlinson, *The Renaissance*, 55.

14. Marin Sanudo, *I Diarii,* R. Fulin et al., ed. (Venice: Visentin, 1879–1903), vol 19, col. 138. Author translation.

CHAPTER 3

Musical Genres of the Renaissance

In this chapter we will take a closer look at the different musical genres that were fashionable during the Renaissance. By "genre" we usually mean a type of music with definite characteristics that distinguish it from other types. The classification of music into separate genres takes into account several factors. One example is the obvious division between sacred music, all the music written for a religious purpose, and secular music, that is, music about any other topic, such as love or politics. Other divisions might take into account the performing medium, for example, distinguishing between solo and ensemble music, or the intended audience, for example, music for the court and music for the public square. Divisions among genres can also be based on other musical and textual characteristics. We will not attempt to explore all Renaissance genres and their subdivisions or make very subtle distinctions; nevertheless, some basic classification, even in a rather general way, is useful to come to grips with this repertory. Only the most important musical genres of the Renaissance will be discussed here, since a more detailed discussion would go beyond the scope of the present book.

Even within a genre, musical style could vary considerably from place to place and from composer to composer. In general, it would be fair to say that the style of sacred music was more international, easily crossing geographical and political boundaries, whereas the style of secular music tended to change from place to place and to reflect more local tastes.

SACRED MUSIC

The Motet

In the Renaissance, a motet could be defined as a sacred composition, usually with a Latin text, for anywhere from three to six voices (although more may be used). Virtually all composers of sacred music in the Renaissance wrote motets. Not all motets were written for the church, however; some were also written to solemnize a particular political event, such as a military victory or the birth of an heir to the throne, but the vast majority set religious texts. There were numerous subgenres of the motet, which are usually classified by the type of liturgical text that is being set to music, for example, a motet that sets the text of a Psalm can be labeled a Psalm-motet. Here we will not be too concerned about these technical distinctions but with the general style and history of the Renaissance motet.

During the Renaissance motets were often the vehicle for musical experimentation and for emotional expression of the text. This happened, in part, because the texts suitable for motets are much more varied than those for the Mass and can be more directly emotional. Motets are usually written in a through-composed form, and this factor also made it possible for the composer to provide music that followed the imagery and sentiments of the text quite closely. Some textual choices were indeed determined by the particular role of a piece of music within the liturgy and were less free, but occasions for hearing motets were much more plentiful than for the Mass, encouraging more freedom in the choice of texts. At the papal court, for example, the pope would hear motets during his supper and not only as part of religious services. This meant that in many cases composers chose texts based on the particular appeal or beauty of a text. One good example can be found in the gorgeous text of the Song of Songs. Even though this biblical passage is full of sensuous references (or perhaps because of that), it crops up frequently in the motet repertory of the period, and its allusions to physical love were consistently interpreted in a symbolic way, for instance, as representing the love of Christ for his Church.

Early Renaissance motets in the "new" style of the period were rather simple, usually in three voices. The greatest change from late medieval examples of this genre was the increased attention paid to the careful setting of the text and the writing of the music so that it was full of consonances (what occasioned contemporaries to stress the "sweetness" of this music). For the largest part of the Renaissance, motets were for four or five voices with an alternation of polyphonic passages in which the voices moved independently to weave a contrapuntal texture, and homophonic passages in which they were locked together to produce a more chordal style. Late Renaissance motets, particularly those of the so-called Venetian School, often came to be written with larger performing forces in mind. These pieces might be written for as many as twelve or even sixteen parts and, in contrast with earlier pieces, they often included written parts for instrumentalists, thus creating a grandiose effect quite unlike that of the simple motets of the early Renaissance.

Countries that broke with the Catholic Church often developed a more distinctive version of the motet. The most important example is that of the Anglican Church, which encouraged the writing of anthems, the counterpart of the Latin motet, using texts in the vernacular. In sixteenth-century England the undisputed masters of their respective generations were Thomas Tallis (ca. 1505–1585), who from 1543 until his death was a Gentleman of the Chapel Royal, and his pupil William Byrd (1543–1623), the most versatile English composer of his day. Both also wrote Latin church music. Byrd, in particular, remained a Catholic all his life, but the protection of Queen Elizabeth avoided any major problems for him and his family, and he was able to continue composition of Catholic Church music in an open manner, as well as secular works and works for the Church of England. The anthems of Tallis tend to be simpler, in the style known as "full anthem"; this is generally a piece for four or five voices, usually without accompaniment, setting a sacred English text in a simple, mostly syllabic, style. During Byrd's lifetime, around 1600, a new and more elaborate style of anthem became popular. Known as "verse anthem," this genre included alternation of solo vocal passages accompanied by instruments with fuller choral passages. Byrd wrote several fine examples of this genre, and he was followed by composers such as Thomas Weelkes (1576–1623) and Orlando Gibbons (1583–1625).

The Mass

The Mass is the central liturgical celebration of the Catholic Church. In monasteries and other religious communities it was celebrated once a day. Laymen were not required to attend Mass daily, but Sunday attendance was expected. The Mass is divided into two parts, the

Ein hüpsch spruch von Kaiser Maximilian.

O Kaiser Maximilian   Dein hohes lob ist nah vnd weit   Viel Künig vnd Kaiser lobenleich
  Dein lob ich nit auß sprechen kan   Du hast erobert viel der streit   In eeren vnd in tugent reich
Waa findt man deins gelaichen.   Vnd deine feind gezwungen   So bist du worden alte
All die mit jr werhafften hand   Shaus Ostereich hast wol bedacht   Das hab du danck du Edler Fürst
Bezwungen hand viel leut vñ Land   Zu eeren vnd groß lob gebracht   Nach Gottes eer hat dich gedürst
  Die müssen dir all weichen   Darauß seind vns entsprungen   Die ist dir yetz behalte,

Antony Formschneider zů Franckfurdt.

Hans Weiditz, *The Emperor Maximilian at Mass.* Emperor Maximilian I (1459–1519) was a great lover of music and spent lavishly on art works. This picture shows a private Mass for the Emperor. On the right, a small choir including boys and adult singers is performing a sacred piece. On the left, a keyboard player is playing a small organ while an assistant pumps the bellows. (Courtesy of Foto Marburg, Art Resource, New York.)

liturgy of the Word, which includes readings from the Old and New Testaments, as well as a homily from the priest and the liturgy of the Eucharist, when the faithful receive communion. Some of the readings and prayers of the Mass are unchanging and remain the same every time a Mass is celebrated. For example, the Kyrie eleison (Lord, have mercy), one of the opening prayers, and the Credo (Creed), the basic statement of the Catholic faith, do not change. Other texts change every day according to the type of feast. These sections will include text that is pertinent to the particular celebration or the saint of the day, often making specific references to the attributes of an individual saint. For example, the Introit to the noon Mass on Christmas Day begins with the words, "For unto us a child is born." This text would not be appropriate for other feasts of the year. We usually call the unchanging texts the Ordinary of the Mass, whereas the changing parts are known as the Proper. Early polyphony written in the Middle Ages tended to set to music texts taken from the changing parts of the liturgy. This suggests that polyphony in that period was an unusual and extraordinary event and not meant for any type of daily use. It is in the fifteenth century, on the other hand, that composers began to adopt consistently the practice of setting the texts of the Ordinary, which had the distinct advantage of being available for use any day of the year. The five parts of the Ordinary that were chosen to be set to polyphony were the Kyrie, Gloria, Credo, Sanctus (Holy, holy, holy), and the Agnus Dei (Lamb of God). When we speak of a polyphonic setting of the Ordinary, we really mean a polyphonic setting of these five movements, which in a Mass occur not as a continuous sequence but at different moments of the service.

The Mass developed quickly into a major musical genre, one that tested the ingenuity and imagination of composers who were constantly producing new musical solutions. Musically, a Mass is not drastically different from other sacred pieces. In the Renaissance, Masses were usually composed for a choir varying from three to six parts (or, rarely, more) in a style that changed according to the generation of composers writing the music. One important advance was brought on by the widespread adoption of Mass settings; almost from the very beginning of the history of this genre, composers began to find musical ways to tie all five movements together. There is no reason for this in the liturgy, nor do we have evidence that this was in any way demanded by church authorities. The monophonic Gregorian chant for the Mass has no ties at all between these movements; in addition, the fact that these movements were not heard as a unit in strict sequence—the way we listen to a symphony in a concert hall—but separated by prayers, readings, and other actions performed during the Mass, means that the reason for these musical links must be a purely artistic one. Obviously, composers must have liked the idea of tying these movements into a unit, because the vast majority of Renaissance Masses do just that.

One type of Mass especially popular in the fifteenth century is known as the cantus firmus (loosely translated: "foundation song") Mass. This means that a composer would select a preexisting monophonic chant (for example, from the liturgical books that held all the chants for the services) then use that tune as the basis for a polyphonic composition. Usually the tune was placed in the tenor, often moving more slowly than the other voices, and the composer would write polyphonic lines to surround it. The additional lines would not normally be musically related to the preexisting tune. The result is a texture that makes it clear to the listener that one voice is different from the others, although it might not be obvious, given the slow rhythms and the presence of other voices, what tune is sung in that particular voice. This is the embodiment of a typical late medieval and early Renaissance frame of mind in which an artist will not make everything obvious to his audience but will try to hide some of the details of the composition. Composers of cantus firmus Masses began quite early in the history of this genre to reuse tunes employed by others. The best known of these tunes is "L'homme armé" ("The Armed Man"), which was popular in the second half of the fifteenth century, and whose form was discussed in chapter 1. Many composers set Masses based on this tune (which, interestingly, was not of a sacred nature), and it seems that part of their delight in using it time and time again was to try and "show up" preceding composers who had dealt with it. In fact, this particular tune remained in use until the end of the sixteenth century, at a time when the original political reasons for introducing it into a Mass would not have been known either to the composers or to their patrons.

Later in the Renaissance, composers sometimes picked an entire polyphonic composition (whether secular or sacred) and used it as a basis for a Mass. Instead of selecting only one voice and writing additional parts, they would choose a composition and retain all voices, usually with small but important changes. This type of Mass is sometimes called a "parody Mass," although in the Renaissance it would have been known as an "imitation Mass." The points made here by the composer in choosing such a procedure could be many: a sort of a game between the composer and a patron, perhaps choosing as a model a piece that the patron liked or a way of showing one's compositional skills, since composers were expected to rework the musical material of the model into a Mass. Other musicians would have certainly appreciated these subtle (and not so subtle) changes, which showed one's ability to manipulate musical material creatively without breaking the rules of composition. In some cases, when two or more composers happened to choose the same model to be arranged into a Mass, there might have been a sense of friendly competition, each trying to be the one with the most imaginative solutions.

Musically, the style of a Mass could vary, not just from composer to composer but even between movements written by the same composer. Three of the movements—the Kyrie Eleison, Sanctus, and Agnus Dei—have relatively little text. For example, the entire text of the Kyrie Eleison consists of the words "Kyrie eleison, Christe eleison, Kyrie eleison" ("Lord, have mercy; Christ, have mercy; Lord, have mercy"), with each invocation repeated three times for a total of nine invocations. In contrast to this, the text of the Credo is rather long, as it lists different items of dogma regarding God the Father, the Son, and the Holy Spirit. When faced with very little text, composers tended to write music in which one syllable would be held over several notes, what we call a melismatic setting. If they had employed a similar procedure for the Gloria and Credo, these movements would have stretched to unacceptable lengths. Thus, composers writing these settings wrote in a much more syllabic style, where for each syllable of the text there is only one note of music, making it possible for the text to be sung much more quickly. In addition, the three shorter texts are usually set in a much more polyphonic texture with a high degree of independence of the individual voices. The longer texts tend to include significant passages in which the voices move all together, enhancing the intelligibility of the text for the audience. Perhaps this was more appropriate, since composers and church authorities wanted to make sure that the basic tenets of the faith included in the Credo would be clearly audible as a reminder to the congregation.

The popularity of the polyphonic Mass waned after the end of the Renaissance. Although it continued to be composed, new styles of sacred music combining instruments and solo voices with choirs became much more appealing to seventeenth-century audiences and obscured the genre that had been so popular for two centuries.

SECULAR MUSIC OF THE FIFTEENTH AND EARLY SIXTEENTH CENTURIES

French Secular Songs

Through most of the fifteenth century the dominant genre of secular music was, by far, the French chanson. "Chanson" is a very generic term that can be applied equally to French medieval songs and French pop music of the twenty-first century. In order to distinguish clearly the fifteenth-century chanson, we often call it "Burgundian chanson," because one of the major centers of this genre was the court of Burgundy in Eastern France. By the fifteenth century, the poetic imagery and forms of chansons of this type already had a long and illustrious history dating from the time of the medieval poet-singers known as trouvères. Textually, the chanson was based on the concept of "courtly love," that is, on poems that treated love in a particularly stylized way. In courtly love chansons, the lover (often a man of noble status) is usually not able to consummate the affair, either because the lady is of a higher social status, already married, or because his love is unrequited. In spite of this, he professes his undying love for his lady and promises to serve her and be faithful all the days of his life. In some more down-to-earth songs, the knight makes very explicit advances to a pretty young lady from the lower classes (a shepherdess is often the object of his attentions) or addresses his friends on some special occasion. Often the texts make allusions to the world of chivalry by talking about knightly deeds. Many of these texts are rather melancholy in nature, full of words such as "anguish," "languish," "pain," "suffering," complaining about love or the vagaries of fortune. We would be mistaken, though, in assuming that these represent the actual feelings of fifteenth-century courtiers. In this period, texts often represent nothing more than an elaborate game in which poets are admired for a clever pun, a new use of an old image, or some other word game. The musical setting was similarly stylized and usually made use of one of the "fixed forms" of the period. These were somewhat complex formal schemes that made a clear emotional relationship between music and text almost impossible. The most common forms of this type were the ballade, popular early in the century; the rondeau, which became the most popular form around 1450; and the virelai.

In spite of all the allusions to suffering included in their texts, these chansons tend to sound, in a sense, generically sad rather than as deep expressions of one's feelings. The most common setting is in three voices, with the melody clearly in the top line and with two supporting lines that might have been played by instruments, at least some of the time, rather than sung. The Burgundian chanson began to lose popularity late in the century, as its audiences became interested in more direct musical expressions of feelings. The most important composers of this genre were Guillaume Dufay (ca. 1398–1474) and Gilles Binchois (ca. 1400–1460).

In this text of a Burgundian chanson (Guillaume Dufay's "Donnes l'assault a la fortresse" ["Attack the fortress"]), note the repetition of large sections of poetry. The music in this piece would have been repeated several times. The first part (number 1 below) is separated into two musical sections, which are usually called A and B, with the break at the first period. Part two also begins with the music of A, but instead of going on to B, it repeats the words and the music of the first A section. Part three repeats the music of part one (AB) but with new text. The last section repeats both the music and the text of the first. The overall musical structure is then AB AA AB AB. This form was known as a rondeau. Notice also the use of imagery from the time of the feudal wars of knights and castles to describe a love affair. The rigid musical forms and the outdated imagery combine to create a sense of distance and slight unreality.

1. *Attack the fortress of my gracious mistress, great god of love, I beg you. Force out my enemy who makes me languish in distress.*
2. *It is for spite that through his roughness he never ceases to injure me before my lady, gentle and joyful. Attack the fortress of my gracious mistress, great god of love, I beg you.*
3. *Come soon to give help, through your nobility, your pity for me, and your courtesy. May the fair one be seized by you, for the delay wounds me deeply.*
4. *Attack the fortress of my gracious mistress, great god of love, I beg you. Force out my enemy who makes me languish in distress.*

Secular Songs in the Late Fifteenth Century

Toward the end of the fifteenth century we begin to see a much more varied landscape in European polyphonic secular music. Several countries begin to develop repertories independent of the French tradition, in fact, often as a form of rejection and opposition to French music.

Most of these repertories have as a distinctive mark a tendency to imitate popular music. This is achieved not only by using actual popular tunes in their music but also by writing texts and music that are simple and express everyday sentiments in a very direct way. Some of these repertories benefited from the invention of music printing from movable type in 1501, which enabled these songs to be printed and sold all over Europe.

The Italian Frottola

"Frottola" is an umbrella term used to indicate a type of Italian song most popular between approximately 1490 and 1520. First cultivated at the sophisticated courts of Mantua and Ferrara, as well as some other Northern Italian courts, the frottola might have been a conscious reaction to the domination of French songs. The most important figure in its development is perhaps Isabella d'Este (1474–1539), born into the ruling family of Ferrara, who in 1490 moved to the court of Mantua when she married Francesco Gonzaga. Isabella, an educated lady who had received musical instruction from the music director of the Este court, had her own household, and she encouraged Italian musicians in her employ to write in this simple style. The most important frottola composers had ties to the courts of Mantua and Ferrara: Marco Cara (ca. 1470–1525) and Bartolomeo Tromboncino (ca. 1470–1535) are without a doubt the most influential of this group. Frottole are usually strophic (as is most popular music) with very clear-cut musical phrases, a definite rhythm, and very simple harmony. They can be found in three-voice versions, with the top line for a voice and the bottom two played by instruments, or in four-voice versions in which all parts can be taken by voices. Sometimes a piece can be found in both versions, and composers seem to have arranged them in either style. Their texts deal with love in a way that differs radically from that of the French chanson. The references to chivalry and the feudal system are gone, replaced by allusions to a more simple life. This was also a game, in a way, since frottole were being produced at some of the most splendid and sophisticated courts of the time where popular sentiments were not likely to be otherwise on display. Later frottole sometimes used better poetry taken from some of the best poets of Italian literature, but the musical settings were limited in expression and were not a good vehicle for the deeper, more personal style that became common in the sixteenth century and that caused the frottole to lose favor. On the other hand, even in the sixteenth century one can find examples of similar types of popular songs composed at a time when the most sophisticated secular music was found in the madrigal.

This frottola text (selected stanzas from Marco Cara's "Mai un muta per effecto" ["One Can Never Change"]) laments the pains of love but with a more realistic and almost cynical point of view compared with that of the Burgundian chanson. One aspect that does not always come through in translation is that the original language sounds much more down to earth than the lofty expressions used in the French Burgundian chansons. Notice the "popular" references in the text. French chanson texts would not have mentioned jackasses and pigs in this way!

Notice also that the first stanza seems shorter. In fact, the first sentence would be repeated, while in subsequent stanzas the music of the first sentence would be repeated with new words. The final sentence of each stanza is the same and uses the same music. This creates a refrain that ties all stanzas together. The second sentence of the first stanza is set to music that contrasts slightly with the music of the opening, while the return of the text at the end brings back the music of the beginning, slightly modified. The overall form is then ABA' (or, more accurately, AABA'). This simple form is still with us in countless popular songs.

1. *One can never change and disguise his true nature. Some people can do no good, but can do evil, and leave everyone dismayed. One can never change and disguise his true nature.*
2. *Every thing must follow its proper nature. There is no art or skill that can turn a falsehood into truth. What is black cannot be white, as our eyes can clearly see. An evil soul does not repent. Time never stops. One can never change and disguise his true nature.*
3. *You can place a nice saddle and bridle on a vile and miserable jackass, but this does not make it into a proud and gentle horse. The pig stays in the sty, because that is its proper place. Fire always gives out heat. Time never stops. One can never change and disguise his true nature.*

Spanish Secular Music

It is in the late fifteenth century that we begin to see a significant repertory of secular Spanish polyphonic music. The court of Ferdinand

and Isabella, proud monarchs of a newly unified Spain, encouraged composers and artists; their music was kept, for the most part, in manuscripts copied for the court. The most important genre of this period is the *villancico*, a type of song very similar to the Italian frottola. Its subject matter is not courtly love but love among common people; it could also be satirical or bawdy. The music is simple, in three or four voices, with frequent repetitions, clear musical phrases, a simple harmony, and a rhythm that often suggests dancing. The strophic settings are typical of popular genres and prevent too close an association between text and music, but they make it possible for the listener to remember the tunes easily through repetition. The melodic lines of the villancico and the frottola are much easier to remember and to sing than those of the Burgundian chanson. Composers such as Juan del Encina (1468–1529/30) composed mostly villancicos, but other genres were also cultivated.

In the sixteenth century, Mateo Flecha the elder (1481–1553) composed several *ensaladas* (literally, salads), pieces whose primary purpose was to imitate the sounds of the real world. His most famous is "La bomba" ("The Pump"), which describes the chaotic scene on a ship caught at sea by a violent storm. Another type of song that can be seen in fifteenth- and sixteenth-century Spain is the romance, a narrative ballad often written for solo voice and accompaniment. The romance has texts that sometimes are more serious than those of villancicos and ensaladas. One surprising fact is that several of these songs set texts that are laments by the last of the Moorish kings who had to leave Granada after the Spanish kings reconquered the last Arab bastion on the European continent. Unusually, these songs present the defeated foe in a rather sympathetic manner.

In this Spanish villancico text (Juan del Encina [1468–1529/30]: "Cucù, Cucù"), the opening line refers to the call of the cuckoo, often used as a symbol of a husband whose wife has been unfaithful. Encina was perhaps the best composer of this genre.

> Cuckoo, cuckoo, cu-cuckoo! Make sure you are not one of them. Friend, you must know that even the best wife is always dying to get it: make sure you really satisfy her!
>
> Cuckoo, cuckoo, cu-cuckoo! Make sure you are not one of them. Friend, you must be watchful, so you are not cheated on: if your wife goes to the outhouse, follow her! Cuckoo, cuckoo, cu-cuckoo! Make sure you are not one of them.

German Songs

The German song (Lied; plural, Lieder) was another genre culti-vated at courts but with a popular bent. The heyday of the Lied was from the fifteenth century to about 1550, and in this period virtu-ally all important German composers had a hand in its success. The two masters of the Lied were Heinrich Isaac (1450–1517), a composer who was Flemish by birth but worked for the Emperor Maximilian I in Austria, and his pupil Ludwig Senfl (ca. 1486–1542/ 43). In their hands the Lied reached the zenith of its popularity. Lieder of this period often used preexisting popular melodies, adapt-ing them in a couple of different ways. One possibility was to use the melody in the top voice and to write two or three more voices in an accompanying role. The settings written in this manner often closely resemble the hymns sung in churches today. One other pos-sibility was to place the melody in a middle voice (usually the tenor) and to write more parts around it, which quite often might have been meant for instrumental performance. The procedure is similar to that used in the cantus firmus Mass, a genre we discussed earlier. The overall effect is one of a vocal melody surrounded by more active instrumental parts, thereby giving it a distinctive sound. There are several examples of one tune being used by the same composer more than once in each of these styles. The texts are usually strophic and turn to popular images to talk about love or, quite often, the plea-sures of springtime. Just as in the case of frottole and *villancicos*, the contrast between the sophisticated courts at which these genres were cultivated and the apparent down-home message of the text must be seen as part of a court game rather than a true taste for popular expression.

The following are two stanzas of a Lied, "Ach Elslein," written by Ludwig Senfl, one of the two masters of the genre. The first stanza is obviously spoken by the man, while the second is the answer of his lover. Direct com-munication of feeling, often with popular sentiments and language, is one of the hallmarks of the Lied.

> *Oh, little Elsa, my dear little Elsa, how would I like to be with you! There are two stretches of deep water between you and me.*
> *This causes me great sorrow, my beloved friend. I say it with my whole heart: it is a great misfortune for me.*

England

In England a fair amount of secular polyphonic music composed during the reign of Henry VIII (1491–1547) has survived. King Henry was quite fond of music and dancing and encouraged these activities. In fact, some of the pieces found in court manuscripts are labeled as having been composed by him, although we cannot be certain that they were. English songs at the court of Henry VIII were also simple, with a strophic text usually in three or four voices and incorporating some popular melody of the time. English songs were not all that was heard at the English court: French vocal music of the period and Italian instrumental music were also heard quite often. The English songs of the court of Henry VIII are not as important as a genre as some of those we have already seen, but they have a certain immediacy and a simplicity that is quite charming.

This anonymous song "And I Were a Maiden" from Henry VIII's book, presents a cautionary tale of the dangers of court life for young, unmarried women. For the courtiers used to the escapades of the king, this must have had particular significance.

It is possible, in fact, that the text would have been interpreted as an allusion to Henry's fifth wife, the young Katherine Howard, who was accused of several premarital (as well as post-marital) liaisons before her execution.

1. *And I were a maiden, as many one is, for all the gold in England I would not do amiss.*
2. *When I was a wanton wench of twelve years of age, the courtiers with their amours they kindled my courage.*
3. *When I was come to the age of fifteen years, in all this land, neither free nor bond, methought I had no peer.*
4. *And I were a maiden, as many one is, for all the gold in England I would not do amiss.*

SECULAR MUSIC OF THE SIXTEENTH CENTURY

The Madrigal

The Italian madrigal is without a doubt the most important secular genre of the sixteenth century, and its influence spread past the Alps to the rest of Europe. The first madrigals were written in Florence and Rome, mostly by foreign composers working for Italian masters in the 1520s and 1530s. The madrigal had some crucial differences from the frottola. Textually, madrigal composers set texts that aspired to be, and sometimes were, of high literary quality. Instead of the simple strophic poems of the frottola, they first turned to the sophisticated poetry of the fourteenth-century poet Petrarch

L. Pozzoserrato, *Outdoor concert*. This is one example of a genre of painting showing ladies and gentlemen of the upper classes playing music in an outdoor setting. It is meant to show the sophistication and breeding of those portrayed. (Courtesy of Scala, Art Resource, New York.)

and to that of those who imitated him in the sixteenth century. As the century progressed, composers also used the most fashionable poetry of their time, for example, excerpts of the epic poem *Jerusalem Delivered* by Torquato Tasso (1581) and of the pastoral play *The Faithful Shepherd* by Giovanni Battista Guarini (1589). In its best examples, this poetry was truly an important window into the human soul, full of opportunities for musical expression with an attention not only to the overall message but also to technical details. Petrarch, for example, was praised by sixteenth-century commentators for his taste and technical virtuosity in choosing words that enhanced the mood of the poem with their sound.

The musical settings were usually in four or five voices, all meant to be sung, and were through-composed without significant repetitions of any musical section. This made it possible for composers to follow the nuances of the text, finding ways to enhance every image and even individual words. For the humanistically trained patrons of the sixteenth century this represented a much more satisfying genre than the frottola, with its wink toward popular culture. This attention to the text is so engrained in the madrigal that we often call its expression "madrigalism" (also known as word painting). Whenever faced with the image of heaven, for example, the music would reach upward; if the image talked about descent into hell, it plunged downward. Mentions of pain and suffering brought dissonances, and a description of bird calls elicited long, florid melodic lines. In the hands of lesser composers, these musical devices turned madrigals into a dry academic exercise, with a paint-by-number feel. Better composers were able to interpret not so much individual words but the whole feeling of the text, enhancing its emotional appeal.

Madrigals remained popular through the sixteenth century and into the first decades of the seventeenth century. During its history the madrigal was often a vehicle for experimentation and innovation. Composers not only responded to new literary tastes, using the most famous poetry of their time, but also to the various debates that explored ways to find adequate musical expression for poetic texts. In fact, one of the most important debates about music around the year 1600 was caused by the appearance of several madrigals by the composer Claudio Monteverdi (1567–1643), which were found by the theorist Giovanni Maria Artusi to be in violation of musical rules. Monteverdi's reply, affirming that the breaking of rules in pursuit of text expression was not wrong, represents the culmination of a period when composers tried increasingly adventurous musical settings for madrigal texts.

Madrigals were often performed in social gatherings. Amateurs getting together for dinner or for an evening of music making could easily perform most of the repertory, at least until late sixteenth-century pieces became increasingly difficult. As music, sophisticated conversation, and the appreciation of good poetry became important social skills, the madrigal provided a perfect medium for the upper middle classes and the nobility to exercise all of those skills.

Early madrigal composers include the Frenchmen Jacques Arcadelt (ca. 1505–1568), Philippe Verdelot (d. before 1552), and the Italian Costanzo Festa (ca. 1490–1545). In the middle of the sixteenth century, as the madrigal began to turn more serious, the Flemish composers Adrian Willaert (ca. 1409–1562) and Cipriano de Rore (1515/16–1565) lead the way with their introspective settings of Petrarch's darker poetry. In the last part of the century the two most successful composers were the Flemish Giaches de Wert (1535–1596), who worked for most of his life at the Italian court of Mantua, and the Italian Luca Marenzio (1553/54–1599). Finally, Claudio Monteverdi represents both a high point of madrigal composition and the end of the polyphonic madrigal.

Somewhat to the side of this line of madrigalists stands one of the most intriguing composers of all times, the Prince Carlo Gesualdo da Venosa (ca. 1561–1613). A nobleman from an important family of the Neapolitan court (he had two cardinals in his immediate family), he was an avid music lover and composer of madrigals marked by extreme dissonance, not seen again in the history of music until the late nineteenth century. Gesualdo is well known to music students for having murdered his first wife, whom he found in bed with her lover. He later married again into the influential Este family of Ferrara, but rumors of mental instability plagued him all his life. Because he was an important nobleman, his daring compositions were not criticized by professional musicians who would have been his social inferiors. His maniacal devotion to music, though, was seen as somewhat inappropriate for a gentleman who was not supposed to be too serious about such a pastime.

These two examples of Italian madrigals span the life of the polyphonic madrigal. The first is from the very first generation of madrigal writing, while the second comes almost at the end of the history of the genre.

This madrigal, "Deh, dimmi Amor" ("Tell me, love"), was published in the first book of madrigals of Jacques Arcadelt, a collection that enjoyed a long-lived popularity, being reprinted well into the seventeenth century. The text is by none other than Michelangelo, who was an accomplished poet, although he is better known as an artist.

Tell me, love, if her soul were as merciful as her face is beautiful, would not every man wish to give himself completely to her? And I, would I not serve her and love her much better if she were friendly to me, since now that she is my enemy I already love her more than I should?

A five-voice musical setting of this madrigal text "Deh, coprite il bel seno!" ("Please, cover your lovely breast!") was composed by Carlo Gesualdo and published in 1611. Typical of his madrigals, the text contains a strong erotic charge and the use of an oxymoron, the pairing of concepts that are apparently mutually exclusive. Many of the madrigals of the time include similar plays on words and a final line with an oxymoron or pun.

The short length of the poem is also typical of late madrigals. Madrigals of the middle of the sixteenth century often set sonnets, or fourteen-line poems.

Please, cover your lovely breast! My soul is dying because of too much gazing. Ah, do not cover it, because my soul, now used to drawing life from that sweetness, hopes, by gazing, to be comforted by that lovely breast that is giving her both death and life.

England: The Madrigal and Other Genres

The success of the Italian madrigal spread to the British Isles, where books of these compositions were imported by local music lovers. The fad for this genre really reached a new level when Nicholas Yonge published *Musica transalpina* (Music from beyond the Alps) in 1588. This was a collection of Italian madrigals whose texts had been translated into English. Previously, English amateurs who wanted to be fashionable had to rely on the original collections with Italian texts. Thus, with few exceptions, they found themselves unable to appreciate the texts of the madrigals, which often included complicated symbolism and rhetorical devices, as important for the enjoyment of the performers as the musical setting. The translations of *Musica transalpina* enabled English music lovers to connect directly with the text and to enjoy its subtleties. Shortly after the publication of this collection, English composers took the final step and began to write new madrigals in English instead of relying on Italian music with an English translation.

In addition to the madrigal proper, English composers also cultivated other types of Italian secular music, copying the style, both in music and text, of their Italian models. Luca Marenzio was particularly admired in England for his elegant madrigal compositions, and the minor composer Giovanni Giacomo Gastoldi was imitated for his balletti, simple pieces with a catchy dance rhythm and nonsense refrains (for example, "fa-la-la") used to set texts talking about love in a carefree and joyous way.

Some of the finest composers of English madrigals were Thomas Weelkes (ca. 1574–1623) and John Wilbye (1574–1638); Thomas Morley (1557/58–1602) was more at ease in the lighter forms. In 1601, however, Morley collected and edited an anthology of madrigals by the title *The Triumphs of Oriana*. The twenty-five madrigals of this anthology, composed by the most important English composers of the time, all set texts in praise of Queen Elizabeth (the Oriana of the title), and each ends with the words "Long live, fair Oriana."

The manual, A Plain and Easy Introduction to Practical Music (1597) in which Thomas Morley talks about secular genres in England, uses large sections taken from Italian treatises and is one of the best known music books of the Renaissance. Morley gives practical instruction in singing and simple composition and discusses the music of his time. This passage deals with secular music in England at the turn of the century, when the popularity of the madrigal was greatest. Notice that Morley seems to condemn the erotic nature of madrigal texts, but this is just an attempt to prevent criticism by the more uptight members of society. The truth is that he did not refrain from using similar texts in his own madrigal compositions.

> *The light [i.e., secular] music hath been of late more deeply dived into, but the best kind of it is termed madrigal: use showeth that it is a kind of music made upon songs and sonnets such as Petrarcha and many other poets of our time have excelled in. This kind of music were not so much disallowable if the poets who compose the ditties would abstain from some obscenities which all honest ears abhor, and sometimes from blasphemies which no man (at least who hath any hope of salvation) can sing without trembling. As for the music, it is next unto the motet the most artificial [i.e., full of "art," "skillful"] and to men of understanding the most delightful. If therefore*

you will compose in this kind, you must possess yourself of an amorous humor so that you must in your music be wavering like the wind, sometimes wanton, sometimes drooping, sometimes grave and staid, otherwhile effeminate; you may show the very uttermost of your variety and the more variety you show the better you will please.

The second degree of gravity in this light music is given to canzonets, that is, little short songs, wherein little art can be showed, being made in strains [i.e., in strophic form].

There is also another kind more light than this which they term balletti, or dances, and are songs which being sung to the ditty [i.e., setting a poem to music] may likewise be danced.[1]

One genre that the Italian-loving Morley fails to mention is perhaps the most English of all secular genres of the Renaissance. Alongside madrigals, balletti, and canzonets, English publishers also issued volumes of pieces that were usually simply called "airs" (or, in the original spelling, "ayres"). "Air" is, of course, a very generic term akin to our "tune" and was not even used exclusively for this repertory, but the genre it describes in this collections is pretty distinctive and typically English. In order to distinguish it from other genres, we usually call it English lute song, although this term is slightly misleading. English lute songs were printed so that several different types of performances were possible. The books usually included parts for four or five voices so that an entirely vocal performance was possible, or there could be a mixture of instruments and voices. They also usually had a part for lute, placed right below the top line (which carried the tune); this made it possible to perform these pieces as solo songs with lute accompaniment. Indeed, it is likely that this version was the one preferred by its composers. The melodies were generally relatively simple but nicely crafted. Lute songs were strophic, but the text of many of these was of a high quality, similar to that of madrigals, and very much unlike that of the lighter secular songs. The best composer of lute songs was John Dowland (1563–1626), a contemporary of Shakespeare and perhaps the best lute player of his generation, and a Catholic in Protestant England. Dowland, an interesting character who also worked as a spy for the English crown, often infused his works with deep feeling and a certain melancholy about the vagaries of life. He sometimes used a Latin motto that punned on his own name: "Semper Dowland, semper dolens," that is, "Always Dowland, always anguished." One of his most famous works in this genre, "Flow, my tears," a somber and haunting piece, was also used by him as the theme for a set of instrumental works and by other composers as a theme for instrumental variations.

Although John Dowland's "Flow my tears" has a dramatic text, not all of Dowland's pieces express such dark sentiments. The success of this piece is perhaps due to the clever way in which the music seems to reflect the text, particularly in the beginning of each stanza. The opening words, "Flow my tears," are set to a descending musical figure that embodies the fall of the tears and also creates immediately a melancholy feeling.

Flow my tears, fall from your springs! Exiled forever, let me mourn; where night's blackbird her sad infamy sings, there let me live forlorn.

Down vain lights, shine you no more! No nights are dark enough for those that in despair their lost fortunes deplore; light doth but shame disclose.

Never may my woes be relieved, since pity is fled, and tears, and sighs, and groans my weary days of all joys have deprived.

From the highest spire of contentment, my fortune is thrown, and fear, and grief, and pain for my deserts are my hopes, since hope is gone.

Hark! you shadows that in darkness dwell, learn to contemn light. Happy, happy they that in hell feel not the world's despite.

France

France in the sixteenth century did not regain the preeminent role it had in the middle of the fifteenth century, when French secular music was the European standard, but continued to produce a repertory of secular songs that was quite popular in Europe. The stylized Burgundian chanson gave way to songs that were either through-composed or with simple strophic forms and that set texts that ranged from high-quality elegies to bawdy, raunchy romps. Already in the late fifteenth centuries, we notice that more chansons abandon the fixed forms of the preceding generation in search of a more direct, simpler expression. The most popular chanson of the sixteenth century is known as the Parisian chanson because most composers and poets of this repertory were based in Paris. It represents perhaps the first repertory to take full advantage of the opportunities offered by the invention of music printing. The Parisian printer Pierre Attaingnant (1494–1551/52) published tens of volumes of chansons, many of which were reprinted several times because of their popularity. Partly because of his success in this area, Attaingnant received the unprecedented honor of being named "royal printer of music" in 1537.

Parisian chansons are usually written for four or five voices, all texted and all moving more or less together (true polyphonic passages are less common), and having a clear, regular melody in the top voice. The effect is similar to that of more popular genres, and these pieces have an immediate charm for the modern listener. Composers include Claudin de Sermisy (ca. 1492–1562), Clément Janequin (ca. 1485–1558), and Pierre Certon (d. 1572). The most important poet for this repertory was Clément Marot (ca. 1496–1544), whose verses have the perfect balance of elegance, direct expression, French wit, and simplicity, shedding the feudal references of earlier chansons in favor of a less archaic vision of love.

Janequin was also famous for his effort in a subgenre of the chanson, which we call the "program chanson," a through-composed piece whose music and text attempt to imitate the sounds of the real world. Janequin composed several pieces in this vein, for example, "Les cris de Paris" ("The market cries of Paris"), "Le chant des oiseaux" ("The song of the birds"), and "Le caquet des femmes" ("The chattering of women"). His most successful program chanson, though, was "La guerre" ("The war"), known also as "The battle of Marignano," which captured in music the sounds of an important battle won by the French King Francis I in 1515. This piece began a fashion for battle pieces, and composers wrote instrumental versions of this piece and even Masses based on the chanson. In one case, a "battle Mass" was deemed appropriate for performance at a service on Mardi Gras.

Later in the century, French composers experimented for a brief period with a style inspired by the desire to imitate antiquity. Composers of this style of chanson set each unaccented syllable of the text with a short note value and each accented syllable with a note value twice as long. The result, known as "musique mesurée à l'antique" ("measured music in the ancient style"), bore little or no resemblance to Ancient Greek models, but it was simple and charming, if short-lived in popularity due to its evident musical limitations.

Clément Janequin's "La guerre" celebrates the victory of the French King Francis I over Imperial troops in a battle fought near Marignano, in northern Italy. Much of the text of the piece reproduces the cries heard in battle ("Courage! Attack!") and its sounds, for example, trumpet calls and the sound of small and large caliber gunfire reproduced by nonsense onomatopoeic syllables ("Von, pa toc pa toc, tric trac, zin zin").

Listen, all you valiant Frenchmen, to the victory of the noble King Francis, and you will hear, if you listen carefully, the strokes given by all sides. Play the pipes, blow! Hit the drums! Turn, maneuver, and change your direction. Brave ones, good friends, cross your staves together; bend your bows, valiant Gascons. Nobles, jump onto your saddles, with the lance ready in your brave hand, like lions. Trombone players, make your sounds! Lively squires, buckle on your weapons, and join the fray. Strike and shout "To arms, to arms." Be brave and joyful, let everyone go forward! The fleur-de-lis, the most noble flower, is there in person [The "fleur-de-lis" is in the coat of arms of the king of France, so this sentence means that the king himself is present]. Follow Francis, the French king, follow the crown. Play the trumpets and the clarions, to cheer up your countrymen.

Fan frere le le fan fan fan feyne fa ri ra ri ra [imitates trumpet calls]

All forward with our standards, move forward the cavalry. Frere le le fan fan fan feyne.

Blast and boom the bombards and cannons, fire the large howitzers and the falcons [types of small cannons] to help our mates. Von pa ti pa toc von von, ta ri ra ri ra ri ra reyne, Pon, pon, pon, pon, la la la, poin poin, la ri le ron.

"France!" "Courage, courage!" Strike your blows! Pa tic pa toc, tricque, trac, zin zin.

Kill! Death! Take courage, hit, kill. Noble gallant ones, be brave, strike, pursue. With your swords, press on. To arms, to arms!

Take courage, pursue them, strike, follow! Our enemies are confused, they are lost, they are showing us their heels. They are fleeing. [Our enemies are saying:] "All is lost." la tintelore. They are defeated. Victory to the noble king Francis! [Our enemies are saying:] "All is lost, by God!"

INSTRUMENTAL MUSIC OF THE FIFTEENTH AND SIXTEENTH CENTURIES

The Fifteenth Century

The Renaissance is the period in which instrumental music begins to move to the forefront of the musical scene. Although still overshadowed by vocal music, instrumental music broke new ground and prepared the important developments of the seventeenth and eighteenth centuries. Much of this development seems to occur in the first half of the sixteenth century, which is perhaps the most crucial period in Renaissance instrumental music. Instrumental music does not begin in this period, but we have very little instrumental music from the Middle Ages and relatively little from the early fifteenth century, especially when we compare numbers with the large vocal repertory available.

The situation begins to change in the second half of the fifteenth century as more instrumental music survives in manuscripts, and some theorists begin to consider practical questions related to instrumental performance. One repertory that survives is German keyboard music, both in manuscripts and in works specifically dedicated to the organ. Most of the pieces are either of the prelude type, used in that capacity before some section of religious services, or some type of arrangement of dance tunes or vocal pieces. Most of these arrangements show one of the voices engaged in faster, virtuosic figurations, either embellishing a dance tune or in contrast to a slow moving liturgical melody. This style of playing would have been easy for organists who were trained from the very beginning in improvising and embellishing musical tunes.

In the late fifteenth century we also see pieces obviously meant for instrumental ensembles. The names given to such pieces can vary tremendously and can be rather generic (e.g., "Piece on A"). Nevertheless, these are some of the first pieces meant specifically to explore instrumental writing without being arrangements of preexisting compositions. By looking at these examples we can see, at least, that composers wrote instrumental melodies in a different way from those of vocal pieces; thus, we can see the beginning of a true idiomatic instrumental style.

One more repertory of instrumental music, that meant for the accompaniment of dancing, is quite important. In the fifteenth century the most popular dance at courts was the so-called "basse danse" ("low dance"), distinguished by a series of somber steps without the kicking of other dances, hence the term "low." We know that an instrumental ensemble of three players usually played these dances, but the manuscripts that include these dances only have the tenor over which the two upper parts would improvise distinct melodies. A few examples do survive in which composers wrote down all the voices, and we have a fairly good idea of how these pieces were supposed to sound. Compared with later dances, their melodic structure is less regular, but dancers of the basse dance relied less on repeated patterns than later dancers. What is important is the role given to these dances in the court life of the period. Paintings and miniatures often show a crowd of young people engaged precisely in this dance, and it is clear that it had a major role in the social entertainment of the period.

The Sixteenth Century

One of the most important changes in the late fifteenth century consisted of a new playing position for the lute, which allowed the player to play more than one string at a time and enabled lute players to be self-sufficient in the way of keyboard players (see more in chapter 5). This opened the gate for a veritable flood of lute music in the sixteenth century: solo pieces, dance music, and arrangements of all kinds of vocal music. By the middle of the sixteenth century the lute was an instrument played not only by professionals but also by a wide range of amateurs, and there is no question that the popularity of this instrument helped the popularity of instrumental music in general. With such an increase in the amount of instrumental music that circulated, several different styles and trends become evident, creating a much more complex landscape than that of the fifteenth century.

When discussing sixteenth-century instrumental music it is easy to get bogged down in making minute distinctions among genres and types of pieces, and this is made even more difficult, and less fruitful, by the fact that often composers of the period were not consistent in applying labels. One more useful distinction, on the other hand, is to divide sixteenth-century instrumental music into broad categories based on their function. These categories are (1) transcriptions and arrangements of vocal pieces; (2) dance music; (3) music for liturgical services; and (4) "pure" instrumental music, that is, music whose sole purpose is the exploration of a compositional or instrumental technique.

Transcriptions and Arrangements of Vocal Music

Until the advent of recorded sound in the twentieth century, transcriptions and arrangements of music (both vocal and instrumental) for different combinations of instruments made up a large and popular repertory. For example, it was common in the nineteenth century to see advertisements for the sale of publications containing arrangements of the most successful pieces from an opera shortly after the opera's premiere. Often these arrangements are somewhat strange (for example, two flutes without accompaniment or bassoon and piano), but we must remember that for many music lovers, perhaps not living close to an opera theater, this was the only way to hear the latest music. It was also a profitable enterprise. Mozart's father pleaded with him to complete his arrangements for wind band of selections from his operas before someone else could beat him to it and corner the market. This practice has a very long tradition, and it is not limited to vocal music: symphonies and string quartets of the time of Beethoven were often arranged for piano four-hands. One of the first manuscripts to include a sizable section dedicated to instrumental music, the fourteenth-century Faenza Codex, contains almost exclusively arrangements or elaborations of vocal music. In the sixteenth century we notice that keyboard and lute collections include a fairly high percentage of arrangements of vocal pieces, which can be either secular songs or pieces of sacred music. The degree to which these arrangements differ from the original may also vary. Some are almost literal note-by-note transcriptions of vocal pieces, but often the texture of vocal music is ill-suited to the instruments. For example, the sounds of the lute fades quite rapidly after a string is struck, so it would be difficult for an exact lute transcription of a vocal piece to retain the effect of sustained long vocal lines. As a result the best arrangers modified the original to take into account the particular qualities of the instruments chosen. For example, pieces with long sustained vocal lines were arranged for lute so that long notes were broken up into faster scale passages that had the double effect of making the arrangement more idiomatic for the instrument and also of giving the performer a chance to show off his or her technique. It is interesting to note that most arrangements and transcriptions used as models some of the most popular vocal pieces of the century. In effect these arrangements show us which pieces were in demand by the music lovers, who were not satisfied with singing them from the vocal part but wanted to be able to play them on their favorite instrument.

In some cases, themes taken from vocal pieces were used in a much freer way, not with the intent of providing a true transcription or arrangement but simply as basic thematic material from which the composer could spin an elaborate composition. These pieces, even though they contain references to the original vocal piece in their title, are much closer to the "pure" instrumental music we will be discussing in the following pages.

Dance Music

Dancing was one of the most popular social activities of the Renaissance, and it should not surprise us that a large number of dance pieces survive from this period. The basse danse, so popular earlier in this period gradually lost its preeminence to other types of dances usually based on regular musical and dancing patterns. Almost anywhere in Europe one finds the pavan (or "pavane"; its name originally meant "from Padua"), a slow, stately dance in duple meter and in many ways the successor of the basse danse. This was often paired with a lighter, faster dance in triple meter that included some high kicking, known as galliard (Italian "gagliarda," meaning robust, lively). Composers sometimes wrote pavan/galliard pairs of dances based on the same theme, tying them together musically. This is the beginning of a trend that will blossom in the late Baroque period, when composers such as Johann Sebastian Bach published suites of contrasting dances, linking together not two but several movements.

Many other dances could be found in Europe at this time. In the late sixteenth century a popular dance at court both in England and France was called "la volta" ("the turn"). The dance was one of the few where the lady and the gentleman danced quite closely, in contrast with other dances where physical contact was limited. It took its name from a characteristic maneuver in which the gentleman would lift a leg, balance the lady on his thigh while lifting her in the air, and execute a three-quarter turn while pivoting on the tip of his other foot. Some of the paintings of this period, capturing the couple in the exact moment when the woman is lifted in the air, show the man with an arm behind her shoulder for balance while his other hand seems to grab her in a daring, risqué manner on her lower torso. In reality that hand is grabbing the bottom of a rigid corset worn by the lady so that the gentleman can more easily lift and balance her. This dance had an obvious potential for disaster in the hands of inexperienced dancers, as the whole maneuver had to be timed precisely to avoid seeing both dancers tumble to the ground.

In addition to pavans and galliards, other popular dances were the branle, the courante, the allemande (the "German" dance), and the high-kicking saltarello. The moresca (Moorish dance) also involved a great deal of physical activity, with leaping and high kicking. Such dances might not have been considered appropriate for all. Baldassare Castiglione, in his book of advice for courtiers, discourages gentlemen from performing spirited dances: "and for all he feeleth himself very nimble and to have time and measure [i.e., a sense of rhythm] at will, yet let him not enter into that swiftness of feat and doubled footings, that we see are very comely in our Barletta [a professional dancer], and peradventure were unseemly for a gentleman."[2]

Castiglione allowed the moresca to be danced only if the gentleman were masked, "because to be in a mask bringeth with it a certain liberty and license." Many other types of dances existed, some only popular in a limited geographical area. Other dances like the "balli," often bearing a distinctive title, were more similar to ballet, as they involved some kind of pantomime in which the dancers performed not only steps but a complex, narrative choreography. We can say that dances like the pavan and galliard could be danced by any number of dancers, whereas the choreographed "balli" were usually meant for a small group (sometimes only a couple).

The sixteenth-century dance music that has survived shows certain fairly constant musical features. First, it is written in strains, that is, repeating musical phrases usually of a predetermined length. This feature was very important because in many of these dances the dancers relied on standard combinations of steps that would require a certain number of musical measures to be accomplished. This was so important that in cases where a composer of dance music used a tune from a vocal piece, he would arrange the tune to conform to the required length of the strain rather than adapting the number of measures of the strain. Second, much of this music looks very simple and does not require a high level of musical skill to be played. This might be due to the fact that this music was published for amateurs. We know that professionals were expected to use these tunes only as basis for embellishment and improvisation, roughly in the way that a jazz player can use an old standard as a springboard for his or her improvisation.

Third, certain types of features are characteristic of a particular dance. Galliards, for example, were in triple meter and also employed a distinct rhythm pattern known as "hemiola," contrasting their typical triple meter with a duple pattern occasionally heard for a short time, especially at cadences. A Renaissance listener would have been very familiar with these sometime subtle differences and would have expected a certain character for a specific dance.

At the turn between the sixteenth and seventeenth centuries, we also see these patterns and characteristics bleed over into vocal music. In Elizabethan and Jacobean England composers sometimes arranged dances as vocal pieces or used dance patterns in composing vocal pieces. In early seventeenth-century Italy similar patterns were taken from popular types of dances and used as the basis for vocal pieces by the best composers. In sum, we can say that dance music had a very important influence on instrumental music of the sixteenth century and helped set patterns that had an effect on the music of successive generations.

Instrumental Music for the Church

The fact that any instrumental music for religious services survives at all is a rather surprising circumstance. The vast majority of instrumental music heard in European churches was organ music, and organists belonged to a select, professional group that relied primarily on improvisation. In the process of auditioning for a church organist position, performers were almost never asked to sight-read a piece from a score or to perform a piece previously memorized. Much of the audition consisted in a series of increasingly complex tests meant to determine whether the organists could improvise and transpose without difficulty. Thus, organists used scores only when accompanying an ensemble but not necessarily when they played solos. Collections of instrumental music sometime included pieces meant to provide a prelude for a section of the liturgy, to introduce a sacred vocal piece, or to fill some of the gaps in the liturgy of the service. The title given to these pieces might vary (prelude, preamble, intonation, and so forth), but their introductory function was clear. Organists also published pieces that were elaborations of Gregorian chants used in the liturgy; other pieces were meant to be played in alternation with the choir, a practice that was quite widespread.

It is unclear as to why these pieces were published at all. Sometimes they were published as part of manuals for the keyboard player. Naturally, a professional organist, trained from an early age in individual lessons with a master, hardly needed these pieces to be written down, but it is possible that a provincial organist at a minor church, somebody who might not have even been a full-time musician, might have benefited from such publications. At the very least, these pieces showed the amateur and less-talented professional how one of the top players might have performed a certain piece. In a sense, these pieces are written-down improvisations rather than compositions in a later sense. Many of them are, in fact, in a rather free form, short, without clear sections, meant to evoke the mood of an improvisation even if they are put down in a score. There were also pieces that were not meant to sound as if improvised but to show the careful contrapuntal working out of themes in a manner reminiscent of a vocal motet. Even these pieces, though, were not very different from what an organist was expected to be able to improvise. Organists were often given a melody and asked to improvise a piece in four parts on the organ, with the original melody being shown successively in all voices and with the proper polyphonic rules observed. What seems to us like an extremely difficult tour de force was, in fact, part of the arsenal of the professional organist.

"Pure" Instrumental Music

Under this category we can group a variety of pieces all sharing the same characteristic, that is, not fulfilling a particular function (such as dance music or music for the church) but meant to serve as a medium for the exploration of compositional and instrumental techniques on the part of the composer. It is in the first half of the sixteenth century that this category of instrumental music seems to undergo a dramatic change. Many terms indicating instrumental genres, never encountered before in the history of instrumental music, appear in this period for the first time. As we can expect, in this case, their relative novelty means that composers did not always use the same terms in precisely the same way, but the important fact is that, as the repertory of "pure" instrumental music expanded, composers recognized that a new category was being developed by coining new terms and names. The following are some of the most important terms:

1. Ricercare: a term derived from an Italian verb meaning "to seek out." First used in a 1507 lute collection to indicate a short, prelude-type piece. Later this term was more commonly applied to a piece where the composer, instead of opting for an improvisatory feel, works out themes in strict counterpoint in the manner of a vocal motet.
2. Canzone: also "canzona," originally meaning a song, first applied to keyboard arrangements of French chansons in 1523; later this became one of the most important types of instrumental ensemble music well into the seventeenth century.
3. Toccata: from the verb "toccare" (literally "to touch" but used both in Italian and Spanish to mean "to play"). First appeared in a collection of lute music in 1536. This term was applied both to lute and keyboard music, usually with the implication that the piece in question is rather free and like an improvisation. Although toccatas have been composed even by contemporary composers, their real popularity lasted until the late Baroque. The organ toccatas of Johann Sebastian Bach remain as monuments of this genre.

4. Fantasia: literally a fantasy, it also first appeared in 1536. The term obviously implies a piece that tests the imagination and cleverness of the performer (and composer, who are often one and the same). Fantasias were written for lute and keyboard and also for instrumental ensembles.

5. Sonata: literally a piece to be played (as opposed to "to be sung"). We find this term for the first time in a collection of music in 1561, but it had been in use before that time. The instrumental sonatas of the late Renaissance, for example those of Giovanni Gabrieli, are very important items in the development of a distinctive instrumental idiom. Originally a rather generic term, it later developed into a highly structured work in the hands of composers such as Mozart and Beethoven.

6. Capriccio: "a fancy." First used in a 1586 collection, this term also implied a certain degree of freedom, almost of whimsy, on the part of the composer. Interestingly, though, some of the early capricci are among the least "free" of the instrumental pieces of the time.

It is certainly significant that so many terms that have played an important part in the history of instrumental music made their first appearance in the Renaissance within a relatively limited span of time. In addition we can find several other terms with a less wide distribution on the European continent. It is noteworthy that many of the terms listed seem to imply that these written-down compositions were supposed to resemble the extemporaneous improvisations for which Renaissance instrumentalists were so famous. With few exceptions (for example, the mid-sixteenth-century ricercare with its strict contrapuntal texture), it is obvious that the sense of freedom, of ideas springing up from the mind of the performer, was very appealing to contemporary audiences.

Another type of instrumental composition that was based on improvisatory practices was the variations set. In it a composer writes increasingly complex embellishments and virtuoso passages based either on a well-known tune or on a repeating pattern of chords—similar, in some ways, to modern-day performers improvising over a blues chord pattern. The names for this type of composition might vary from country to country (e.g., divisions in England, diferencias in Spain), but the concept was something that instrumentalists learned at the same time as they learned their instrument. In fact, many of the sixteenth-century manuals on instrumental performance include sizable sections dedicated to the practice of extemporized embellishment and variation, complete with tables showing the student how to break down and embellish simple melodic patterns commonly found in music of the time.

"Pure" instrumental music made tremendous strides in the sixteenth century. We could argue that by the last decades of the century, instrumental compositions such as canzoni and sonate were even influencing the style of the sacred music of some composers. Particularly in the use of distinctive and memorable rhythms, of shorter melodic themes, and of a clearer and more "modern" harmony, there is no doubt that the lessons of instrumental music spilled into the vocal repertory. Most chord patterns used for instrumental improvisation, for example, are very simple and closer to patterns found in modern pop songs than to the harmonies found in a polyphonic motet. It is this "modern" use of harmony that becomes more common in vocal music of the early seventeenth century and paves the way for the modern system of harmony that was so fully embraced by the likes of Mozart.

The following passage, about a sixteenth-century star performer and his audience, was written by a Frenchman, Jacques Descartes de Ventemille, who was visiting Milan in northern Italy and had the good fortune to hear the great lute player Francesco Canova da Milano (1497–1543) perform for the guests at a banquet. Notice that the traveler stresses the improvisational nature of Francesco's playing. No score is needed for this type of solo performance. The type of exclusive attention given by the audience to the performer is something we take for granted in a modern concert hall but this was, in fact, rather exceptional in the Renaissance. Instrumentalists and singers are often shown performing at a gathering, while the "audience" is engaged in all sorts of activities while listening. Even accounting for the typical Renaissance flowery prose, it is obvious that the writer was deeply impressed by Francesco's performance.

The tables being cleared [Francesco] chose one, and as if tuning his strings, sat on the end of the table seeking out a fantasia. He had barely disturbed the air with three strummed chords when he interrupted the conversation that had started among the guests. Having constrained them to face him, he continued with such ravishing skill that little by little, making the strings languish under his fingers in his sublime way, he transported all those who were listening into so pleasurable a melancholy that—one leaning his head on his hand supported by his elbow, and another sprawling with his limbs in careless deportment, with gaping mouth and more than half-closed eyes, glued (one would judge) to the strings of the lute, and his chin fallen on his breast, concealing his countenance with the saddest taciturnity ever seen—they remained deprived of all senses save that of hearing, as if the spirit, having abandoned all the seats of the senses, had retired to the ears in order to enjoy the more at its ease so ravishing a harmony; and I believe we would be there still, had [Francesco] not himself—I know not how— changing his style of playing with a gentle force, returned the spirit and the senses to the place from which he had stolen them, not without leaving as much astonishment in each of us as we had been elevated by an ecstatic transport of some divine frenzy.[3]

NOTES

1. Thomas Morley, *A Plain and Easy Introduction to Practical Music*, 2d ed., ed. by R. Alec Harman (New York: Norton, 1973), 294–5.

2. Castiglione, *The Courtier*, 105.

3. Translated by Joel E. Newman, and quoted in Arthur J. Ness, *The Lute Music of Francesco Canova da Milano (1497–1543)* (Cambridge, Mass.: Harvard University Press, 1970), 2.

CHAPTER 4

Music and Dance in Renaissance Society

In this chapter we will see how the music we have discussed so far was used in different social contexts during the Renaissance. Music in all societies generally serves a variety of functions: it can be used as entertainment, as political or military propaganda, as an ornament to religious services, as a subversive statement, as a sign of culture and sophistication on the part of the listeners, as an important part of courting rituals, as an accompaniment to work routines, and even as a way to spread news in an era without mass media. Even though music is much more of a presence in today's society, thanks to radio, television, movies, and CDs, it would be a mistake to assume that there was little music in the sonic landscape of Renaissance life. Dance also had important functions beyond pure entertainment, to the point that a Renaissance commentator was moved to write that dancing was "essential to a well-ordered society."[1] Let us now look at different ways in which music and dance were employed to fulfill some of those functions.

MUSIC IN THE STREET

The music that was probably heard in the streets of Renaissance cities and in the countryside, the repertory that was most familiar to the average person, is also the music that has left fewer traces. Most folk musicians did not need the ability to write their music down, because the oral tradition of which they were part taught them to memorize a large number of pieces. As in the folk music of today, much folk music was probably written according to formulae (that is,

Albrecht Dürer, *The Dance, The Bagpiper*. (Courtesy of Giraudon, Art Resource, New York.)

musical and textual patterns that can be easily adapted and rearranged to form new pieces). When we think of the thousands of pieces that have been written using the standard blues form as a springboard, we begin to understand how folk music worked in the Renaissance. The existence of readily available, standardized patterns would have enabled folk musicians (not necessarily professionals) to make up new songs and tunes rather quickly. The Florentine chronicles report that after an unsuccessful conspiracy against the ruling Medici family in the fifteenth century, the mob carrying the body of a conspirator (to dump it in the Arno river) made up a "strambotto" (a type of poem often set to music) about the events of the day. Traces of these traditions can be observed in many European folk traditions of today, for example, in musical "contexts" where two performers will sing alternate stanzas of a song, responding to one another and trying to "win" by being the cleverest and funniest. Incidentally, this is a tradition that once was also found in "art" music, at least since the time of the troubadours in eleventh- and twelfth-century France.

Not all music that was heard at the time was music in the sense that we usually define it. City markets resonated with the cries of the sellers hawking their wares, falling into a sing-song musical rhythm as they did so. We can still experience this today in most markets of cities all over the world, and the experience is as powerful today as it must have been in the Renaissance. Composers themselves were not deaf to the possibilities of this street music. From the late Middle Ages, when Francesco Landini (d. 1397) wrote a piece re-creating the market cries of Florence, to the sixteenth century, when the French composer Clément Janequin (d. 1558) published his "Les crys de Paris" ("The market cries of Paris"), several pieces were written to capture the music of the street market in a more sophisticated composition.

It was probably also quite common to hear music sung or played by various types of beggars in the streets of the city and, once again, it would be hard for us to know exactly what was being performed. It would be wrong, though, to assume that all street music must have been folk music. From later centuries we have plenty of examples of successful art music being performed in much more informal situations. In nineteenth-century Italy, for example, not long after the premiere of an opera, the most successful arias could be heard in the mouths of lower class servants in the streets. It is possible that some of the music heard in the streets of Renaissance cities might also have been "recycled" art music, first heard in the palaces of the rich.

One particular category of street performers active in the Renaissance was part of a rich tradition that continued in Europe well into the twentieth century and began to decline only when mass entertainment became available through radio, television, and movies. In almost every main square of Renaissance cities one could see itinerant street performers engaged in a wide variety of activities. They would dance and tumble, do magic tricks, perform some type of semi-improvised comic skit, and sing. The names by which they were known changed from place to place. In Florence, for example, they were known as "cantainbanchi" (literally, those who sing on a table) from the practice of setting up a makeshift platform in the square so the performers could climb on it and be seen by a larger crowd. Their craft was often regulated by the authorities who required them to acquire special permits in order to perform, and their profits came, as it were, from "passing the hat" among the crowds that gathered. Besides entertainment, some of them provided another valuable social function as a sort of storytellers. Their storytelling was accompanied by music, as is evident by another of their names, "cantastorie" (that is, he who sings stories), and the stories told could range from retelling of old legends to topics taken from recent history and current events. In some small towns and villages in Europe this practice was still very much alive at least until the middle of the twentieth century. The storyteller would often use a series of roughly painted images to help him narrate the story, and he would use well-known poetic and musical patterns, transmitted from generation to generation, to set the story to music. In a society where literacy was not widespread and, at any rate, there were no newspapers, the storytellers probably provided a great deal of the information the lower classes received about the world outside their immediate surroundings.

Another type of music that was probably quite commonly heard is what was sung by workers engaged in different activities. Some of this music had a very practical application: It enabled workers doing difficult manual labor to coordinate their efforts, for example, in pulling a heavy load or manning a winch. Work songs of this kind are still very much in use throughout the globe today, and sometimes they could be suggested by the rhythm of the work activity. Commercial fishermen fishing with nets often used rhythmic beats (for example, beating the oars against the side of the boat to scare fish toward the waiting nets) and accompanied the rhythmic noise with songs. Songs like this survive today in folk traditions, and it is easy to see how the rhythmic beating of the oar might have suggested to the fishermen the singing of a song to accompany it. In other cases it was probably just a way to ease the monotony of repetitive tasks and to pass the time.

There was one other way in which music was used by the lower classes, especially in the countryside, and that was to accompany magic rites. In spite of the fact that Europe had been Christianized for centuries, in many cases local pagan rites survived. These were not necessarily malevolent; in fact, many of the gatherings (some secret, some not) were of what we would call the "white magic" variety, that is, the performance of rites intended to ensure a bountiful harvest, the arrival of sufficient rains, the health of farm animals, and so on. From the documents left by the tribunals of the Inquisition, which tended to take a dim view of such practices, we know that those who participated would feel quite often that they were performing a service essential to the community.[2] These gatherings would often include music and dancing, not surprising since these activities have been linked with magic since earliest recorded history. At all levels of society, for example, there was a belief in the powers of music to influence behavior and to heal the sick, and the fact that music was used in any kind of magic rite is perfectly in line with those beliefs.

Finally, of course, music and dancing were used by the lower classes also for entertainment. Popular dance halls were found in most cities, and anyone could gain admission there by paying a small fee, but dancing occurred more informally at various gatherings, celebrations, and festivals. Singing and playing also occurred independently of dancing, and usually the performers would be amateurs or semiprofessionals at best, musicians who spent most of their time engaged in other activities. Occasionally, while going through Renaissance legal and official documents, one finds references to individuals identified as "carpenter and musician," "bookseller and musician," or even more colorfully in one case, as "Nicholas of the harpsichords, who goes out to sea as helmsman, nicknamed 'half-dog'." These individuals either did not possess the skills to make it into the competitive professional musical world or were barred from it because of the rather close-knit associations among professional musicians, which tended to favor friends and relatives over outsiders.

Although virtually no music survives from these popular gatherings, we can arrive at some conclusions based on evidence from numerous prints and paintings, and on the popular tunes that composers of art music sometimes incorporated into their pieces. From this scant evidence we can say that popular pieces were often organized in a simple, straightforward manner with clear-cut musical phrases and a very definite rhythmic feel, even at the time when these characteristics were not normally found in the music of the upper classes. Even without having much detail on the actual music heard in the streets of European cities and towns, though, we can surely say that music was often present and that the ingenuity of the population found many ways to incorporate music in daily life.

MUSIC AT COURT

At the other end of the spectrum from the streets stand the splendid courts of the Renaissance. As we have seen, in the Renaissance large parts of Europe were divided into relatively small states, even city-states, often ruled by a succession of hereditary rulers. This situation was especially obvious in Italy where within a rather small geographical area one could find several wealthy and sophisticated courts. Just within northern Italy, going no farther south than Florence, are the courts of Florence, Mantua, Ferrara, Venice, and Milan, in addition to many other less important states. Each one of these courts was in direct competition not only for political and territorial gains but also for the admiration and praise of their contemporaries as models of refinement and sophistication, as shown in their expenditures for new buildings, decoration, statues, paintings, elaborate gardens, and in their patronage of artists and writers.

Courts had the financial resources to hire and retain groups of professional musicians, to purchase and maintain expensive instruments, to commission the copying of music manuscripts (some very elaborate), to buy printed music, and to provide adequate performance spaces.

Musicians would be listed among court employees and were generally expected to abide by the same restrictions as other court officials. Depending on the court, there could be several layers of supervision between the musician and the ruler, but the fact that musicians were expected to perform before the ruler and his or her circle meant also that professional musicians had access to the ruler that was denied to others. Musicians could be listed in different sections of a court payroll depending on their function at court. In general, a ruler was expected to maintain a church choir and organist for his private chapel, a group of instrumentalists and singers to provide chamber

Hans Burgkmair. From *The Triumph of Maximilian I*, "Sweet melody." This is part of a set of 137 woodcuts commissioned by the Emperor Maximilian I. This woodcut shows the chamber musicians of the Emperor. It includes wind and string instruments suitable for chamber performances. The last musician on the right is playing a pipe and tabor, that is a recorder with one hand and a drum with the other, the one-man dance band of the Renaissance. (Courtesy of Dover.)

music, and a group of wind players and trumpeters to accompany him (or her) when participating in processions or other ceremonies, or when leading the army. Thus sizable resources were devoted to music.

The court of the French king Francis I in the early sixteenth century divided its musicians between the choir for sacred music (the chapel) with around twenty-four members, the musicians of the chamber (that is, a smaller number of singers, lute players, keyboard players, and viol players), and the Ecurie (literally, the stable), which included as many as twelve trumpeters and eight players of loud wind instruments. The much smaller court of Ferrara in 1476 employed thirty-seven musicians, divided as follows: four ceremonial wind instrument players, four trumpeters, eight singers and players for secular music, twenty singers for the chapel, and one church organist.[3] Figures from some north Italian courts of the late fifteenth century show expenditures for music rising and, in some cases, reaching more than five percent of total court revenues. In addition to regular salaries, musicians of the court often received official governmental appointments, tax exemptions, and various gifts.

The resources available for music, though, might not have been sufficient to support the types of musical establishments found at Renaissance courts had it not been for a Renaissance sense that a ruler had to be more than a good military leader and a capable manager. He also had to be a cultivated individual, at ease among artists, able to compose poetry, sing, play, dance, carry on a good conversation on a variety of topics, and read ancient and contemporary authors and philosophers: in sum, a well-rounded individual. Thus these qualities became desirable throughout the aristocracy and also among the upper middle classes who, having now more money and leisure than ever before, began to imitate the example of the nobility. We can say that many of the prominent aristocrats of the Renaissance were praised as much for their patronage of art and artists and for their personal knowledge of all fine arts and literature as for their military or political skills. Prince Juan of Castille, the heir to Queen Isabella, took such pleasure in singing in a small group that, although his voice was said to be rather unexceptional, almost every day after lunch he had the choirmaster of the royal chapel and a few singers come to the palace where "the prince sang with them for two hours, or however long he pleased to, and he took the tenor, and he was very skillful in the art."[4] Emperor Charles V of Spain was said to be so well trained in music that he could tell when his singers sang a wrong note, and he would reprimand them when they made mistakes. Naturally, we never know in these situations whether the praises of the ability of a ruler are honest or simply an attempt to curry favor, but the fact that these qualities were praised means that they were seen as desirable.

As a result, rulers of the period spent very large sums of money on the arts, although, to be fair, equally large sums could be spent on their horses or hunting falcons. Some were so fond of the arts and other entertainments that they were sometimes criticized for not paying sufficient attention to the affairs of state. When Duke Vincenzo Gonzaga of Mantua died on February 18, 1612, for example, he left his heir Francesco a financial mess caused by many years of profligate spending in many areas, including music. Duke Vincenzo, himself an amateur composer, had succeeded in creating one of the most splendid musical establishments in all of Europe but at a staggering financial price. Important rulers like Duke Vincenzo seem to have spent a great deal of effort and money on music, and it is obvious that they were highly competitive about it. Vincenzo's counterpart at the northern Italian court of Ferrara, Duke Alfonso d'Este, organized the first group of professional women singers used primarily for private concerts in the ducal apartments. He was so involved in their music that a contemporary observer wrote: "The Duke is so inclined to and absorbed in this thing [i.e., music by female singers] that he appears to place there not only all his delight but also the sum total of his attention. One cannot give him greater pleasure than by appreciating and praising his ladies."[5] This pleasure was denied to him when he had this group perform for his friend and rival Vincenzo Gonzaga and asked him his opinion about the performance. Duke Vincenzo responded quite inappropriately with a derogatory comment on women in general, saying, "I'd rather be a jackass than a woman." Yet within a short period of time, Duke Vincenzo hired and retained women singers at his court and was inordinately proud of their achievements, showing that his rude comment was simply a case of sour grapes.

We know from the *Book of the Courtier*, by Baldassare Castiglione, that gentlemen and ladies were expected to have musical and dancing skills. He lists as desirable musical skills the ability to sing a piece of music at sight; performance skills on lutes, viols, and keyboard instruments; and especially the performance of a solo voice accompanied by a single lute "singing almost as if reciting." The performances by amateur aristocrats were also limited by many rules of decorum. Among other rules, aristocrats were not to perform in front of their social inferiors and older noblemen were not supposed to sing love songs in any kind of gathering. In Castiglione's words:

> But the seasoning of the whole must be discretion . . . and if the Courtier be a righteous judge of himself, he shall apply himself well enough to the time, and shall discern when the hearers' minds are disposed to give ear and when they are not. He shall know his age, for, to say the truth, it were no meet matter, but an ill sight, to see a man of any estimation being old and gray, toothless, full of wrinkles, with a lute in his arms playing upon it, and singing in the midst of a company of women, although he could do it reasonably well. And that, because such songs contain in them words of love, and in old men love is a thing to be jested at.[6]

This idealized view of the skills of courtiers in musical matters might not have always corresponded to reality, but an aristocrat of the Renaissance could have pointed to many examples of the embodiment of those principles. King Henry VIII of England, for example, was described in 1515 as able to play almost every instrument, to compose songs, and to sing "from a book at first sight." Far from being in his youth the bloated monarch we usually remember from later portraits, Henry was also a good dancer and an athlete, with his im-

Hans Holbein the Younger, *The ambassadors*. This portrait of the French ambassador to the court of King Henry VIII, Jean de Dinteville (left) and his friend Georges de Selve includes several signs of their rank, from the opulent clothes they wear, to the scientific instruments on the top shelves (a sign of learning), to the musical instruments and music books that are shown on the shelves (some barely visible). The strange shape at the bottom of the portrait, when viewed from an appropriate angle, reveals itself to be a skull, an admonishment to all that this wealth is transitory. (Courtesy of Alinari, Art Resource, New York.)

posing six-foot two-inch frame and a thirty-five-inch waist, at a time
when average heights were much shorter than today.

A court could be judged by outsiders as much on the grace and
skills of gentlemen and ladies in singing and dancing as on other, more
important, traits. It was not uncommon for courtiers to take part in
performances honoring an important guest of the court or simply
providing entertainment at nightly gatherings. Many Renaissance nar-
ratives of life at court, or among aristocrats, often conclude an
evening's pastimes with a dance performed by those present, sometimes without any instrumental accompaniment but simply by singing a dance tune while dancing. Dance masters and music masters were
usually present at courts, and dance masters provided choreographies
for more elaborate dances and displays as well as individual instruction in the kind of dances in which most of the courtiers would participate. Choreographed dances could be rather elaborate and even
whimsical, often introducing characters from far-away places, dancing
and creating a pantomime around some fanciful narrative.

An interesting case of a very elaborate entertainment performed
mostly by gentlemen and ladies is a wedding dinner and reception that
took place in 1513 in Venice. The bride and groom were from two
of the most important families of the city; in fact, the bride was the
niece of the ruling *doge* (duke), and the families made sure this was
going to be a memorable occasion. After a dinner served to 420 guests,
which included ambassadors respectively from the Pope, the Emperor
of Spain, and the Holy Roman Emperor, among other noble guests,
the entertainment began, sponsored by the friends of the groom who
belonged to the same *compagnia della calza* (a type of "club" for
young aristocrats):

> Then they began preparations to recite a comedy or certain entertain-
> ments, and they had prepared a stage for the women and another in the
> middle of the hall to recite the said thing. And on this stage sat down
> the "king" of the *compagnia* known as "the Eternals": many of the
> *compagni* [i.e., the members of the *compagnia*] danced for a while with
> the women, then the first scene began. First came Sir Marco Antonio
> Memo, and he presented to his "king" a papal brief, pretending that
> the Pope was sending him, the bishop of the hoboes, to present his good
> wishes. The "king" thanked him and ordered to see some dancing, and
> on the other stage there was a dance by two young ladies and two of
> the young gentlemen. After the dance the false papal ambassador had
> everybody listen to one of his employees, Galeazzo del Valle, who im-
> provised some songs accompanying himself on the lira da braccio. And

later Sir Giovanni Cavalli came, dressed as the Imperial ambassador, and there were some dances performed by two ladies. And the [fake] ambassador had his musicians play some music with flutes and wind instruments. After this, Sir Santo Contarini showed up dressed as a Mameluke, that is the ambassador of the Sultan. After another dance by the ladies, the ambassador had his servants dance a Moorish dance. Then came the ambassador of France, played by Sir Giovanni Contarini, and after the ladies' dance, he had cornetti and trombones play. Then the Spanish ambassador, and there was another dance done by ladies. Then the ambassador of Hungary, who was played by the groom, and after another dance he had his "Hungarians" play a small viol and some other instruments. Then there was the ambassador of the Pigmies and after the dance by the ladies, he had his four Pigmies dance well with axes in their hands and in quadruple meter. Then there were three Venetian ambassadors, and after the dance of the ladies, there was some impressive tumbling by two servants, and four peasants sang some songs.[7]

This rather elaborate description, which is fairly typical of its type, also shows some of the problems faced by historians trying to collect information on music in the Renaissance from similar documents. The reader will quickly notice that very little specific information is given here about the music or the dancing. There are some mentions of instruments, but not necessarily useful to re-create the music performed. There is one musical indication in the whole passage, which describes the dance of the Pigmies as being in quadruple meter. In spite of the fact that the observer, the nobleman Marin Sanudo, was a very educated and cultivated individual, not a single piece of music is identified by title. Only one dance is identified by type, the Moorish dance (*moresca*), but most of the dances are simply mentioned without further comment. It is very difficult to know exactly what was being played, sung, or danced. Even some relatively straightforward comments are not so simple to interpret. The ladies dancing were members of the aristocracy, but, for example, who were the "servants" who played some of the music? Were they professional musicians actually employed by the noblemen or amateurs who pretended to be the servants of the fake "ambassadors" in the general playful mood? Were those real peasants or young aristocrats masquerading as such? In conclusion, all we can really say about an event like this one is that music and dance occupied a central position in festivities sufficiently important to gather together virtually all of the ruling class of Venice and several honored guests. We can notice the considerable effort made to create a varied and interesting, even extravagant, spectacle, but if we were asked to re-create that particular event today, we would have very little musical information at hand.

For elaborate entertainments involving music, few courts could compare with that of the Dukes of Burgundy. The court of Burgundy was, in many ways, the most splendid court of the fifteenth century, benefiting from its control of some of the wealthiest cities of northern Europe. The most famous of the dukes was Philip the Good (d. 1467), who was interested in establishing Burgundy as the grandest court of all Western Europe. When the city of Constantinople (modern-day Instanbul) was conquered by the Ottoman Turks in 1453, Philip broadcast a call to organize the flower of Western chivalry in a crusade to retake the city. He revitalized a chivalric order founded in Burgundy in 1429, the Order of the Golden Fleece, to achieve that aim. Although the crusade never materialized, the order did manage to have regular yearly meetings, which usually included elaborate ceremonies. The most elaborate of these meetings was perhaps the one when the assembled knights took an oath to seize Constantinople back from the Turks. The grandiose feast that culminated the proceedings on February 17, 1454, is known as the Banquet of the Oath of the Pheasant, and it involved extremely elaborate displays of music and pageantry. This is a case of music and the arts in service of political aims, as the celebrations surrounding the establishment of the Order of the Golden Fleece were meant to position the Duke of Burgundy as the defender of Christianity and the true heir to the knights of the past. Virtually anything that was performed during the banquet had some type of significance that would have been much more vivid to the invited guests. Nevertheless, we learn quite a bit from the description written by the court official Olivier de la Marche. His description, similar to the one cited above, does not include titles of compositions, with two exceptions, and does not tell us much about the music played. It does often refer to an instrument being played "in a new way," but then the writer does not explain what that particular "new way" might be. We are struck, however, by the sheer complexity of these proceedings. The evening revolved around a number of short staged scenes, all of them with symbolic meaning. They began with the story of Jason, the mythological Greek hero credited with the theft of the Golden Fleece, and ended with a scene in which a female singer, representing the Church and arriving on top of an elephant led by a "huge giant," sang a lament for the loss of Constantinople. In between these short scenes there were musical interludes and other actions. In the middle of a large hall there were three stages of varying size. On the small one there was a "marvelous forest, like a forest of India," with a variety of animals and birds that "moved by themselves, as if alive." On the medium stage was a skillful model of a church, with four singers inside and a working bell. On the largest, de la Marche describes a huge cake with twenty-eight musicians playing various instruments.

Notice, incidentally, that de la Marche could not have possibly known what a "forest of India" looked like and that he is simply describing something that to him seemed magical and strange. Here is a small part of the description of the activities at the banquet that will give an idea of how far the Duke went in trying to have a spectacle of unsurpassed splendor:

> First, as soon as everyone was seated at the table, in the church [i.e., the model of a church] a loud bell rang, and after that bell stopped, three little choirboys and a tenor began to sing a very sweet chanson; what the song was, I would not know, but I thought for my part that it was a very pleasant blessing to begin the banquet. After those in the church finished, a shepherd played a bagpipe in a very new way. Right after that, through the entrance to the room, a horse came in walking backwards, and on that horse there were two trumpeters and they played a fanfare on their trumpets. After the church and the cake had each played four times, from the door came into the hall a stag, marvelously large and beautiful, and on the stag rode a twelve-year-old boy, and when he entered the room the said boy began to sing very loud and clear the upper part of a chanson, and the stag sang the tenor, without anyone else being visible, beside the boy and the artificial stag, and the song they sang is called "Je ne vis onques la pareille" [I have never seen the equal].[8]

Everything in this description is meant to impress the reader with the magnificence of the court, from the mention of the twenty-eight musicians in the cake, at a time when very few courts could have even put together such a large number of instrumentalists, to the unusual presentation of the trumpet fanfare and the chanson sung by the "stag." Whether the duke liked music or not (although we know he did) is somewhat irrelevant. What the guests were supposed to take home with them from this event was an admiration for his court and perhaps a sense of respect for his financial power, which, of course, could be easily translated into military power. These types of entertainments can be found throughout the Renaissance at various courts. Later in this period, courts sometimes published not only a description of the events but also the scores of the music heard there, primarily because this was supposed to widen the circle of those who could then marvel at the magnificence of the court.

In the later part of the sixteenth century, a type of musical entertainment often performed at court would be the *intermedio*, a presentation that included music, costumes, special effects, and dancing, performed in between the acts of a staged play. In many cases, *intermedi* became almost as long and more elaborate than the play they were supposed to accompany, and courts vied with one another to stage ever more splendid presentations. A famous set of *intermedi* was performed at the northern Italian court of Mantua in 1598, between the acts of *Il pastor fido* ("The faithful shepherd"), perhaps the most famous play of the late sixteenth century. The *intermedi* honored Margaret of Austria, the recently wedded bride of Philip III of Spain, with allusions to the mythical wedding of the god Mercury with Philology. Here is part of the detailed description of the event, which comprised a prologue, four intermedi, and a final farewell scene:

> At the beginning, when the curtain was raised, one could see the city of Mantua and a cloud in the sky, on which Venus was seated, with the star Espero to the right and the star Giulia to the left, and those three together sang a madrigal in honor of Her Majesty the Queen [Margaret]. . . .
>
> After the third act [of the play] we heard the sound of drums coming from underground, and in the meantime the stage became all full of very high mountains, and all of sudden we saw many savage deities come out with various musical instruments. At the same time we saw a chariot pulled by lions come out from under the earth, amidst the playing of drums, and the mother of all gods was on it, and with a drum in her hand she was making that sound. . . .
>
> At the end of the pastoral play, the sky opened up everywhere and one could see all the gods in their proper places, scattered among the shiniest clouds, with the bride and groom on the throne of Jupiter, while the shepherds on the stage began to sing . . . at that point the gods who were with Hymeneus [god of marriages] with a new music, almost showing a new ballet, had the dancers come out on the scene, and the dancers, first with drums and drumsticks, then with the arrows of the shepherds, and later with the torches of the same [shepherds] danced a three-part *moresca* [a lively dance], filling the air with sweet smell of their fire.[9]

We can imagine the reactions of the audience to this amazing display of special effects, dancing, music, and staging. In fact, these *intermedi* contained many more special theatrical effects than the main play, and it is obvious that the purpose of their staging was to show the audience the magnificence of a court that could afford such a spectacle.

Of course, music was also heard at court on a more private basis, for dancing, singing, and playing were considered honest pastimes and perfectly appropriate for the nobility. These were not performances, in the later sense of professionals performing for an audience, but occasions where the performers entertained themselves and one another. There were also sometimes other reasons why it was important for the courtiers to know music and dance. Queen Elizabeth of England was, as we have seen, a great lover of music and dance, to the point that the French ambassador recorded in one of his dispatches that "she takes great pleasure in it [dancing] that when her maids dance she follows the cadence with her head, hand and foot. She rebukes them if they do not dance to her liking, and without a doubt she is mistress of the art."[10] Elizabeth was herself a lover of dancing, but in 1598 it would not have been appropriate for the aging queen to dance in front of other courtiers. Skill in dancing, though, gave courtiers a chance to get closer to the monarch. An account written by a German traveler in 1585 describes in some detail a slow, dignified dance performed in front of the queen "only by the most eminent who were no longer very young." After this dance, the younger courtiers took off their jackets and cloaks and began to dance a more spirited dance: "They danced the galliard, and the Queen meanwhile conversed with those who had danced. The dancing over, the Queen waved her hand to those present and retired to her chamber. But as long as the dancing lasted she summoned young and old and spoke continuously."[11] Obviously, in this case, the ability to dance in front of Elizabeth meant that the aristocrat could also gain access to the queen, exchange a few words, and perhaps petition for a favor.

CITIES WITHOUT A COURT

Many of the wealthiest cities in Europe in the Renaissance were not governed by an absolute, hereditary ruler but had a more democratic form of government. Very few of these cities could be described as democracies in the modern sense, and many, in fact, were technically under royal or imperial jurisdiction, but the actual government was carried out by some type of elected council (although universal suffrage was unknown), and such cities did not have at their center an aristocratic court. The negative implication for music of arrangements of this type is that there would not be a single patron willing to spend extravagant sums of money on music, but, on the positive side, musicians who served there would have terms of service less dependent on the whims and vagaries of the court and its ruler. Cities such as Antwerp, Lyons, fifteenth-century Florence, Venice, and Nuremberg were as full of music as any court city, but the ways in which music was produced and heard varied considerably. Some groups of musicians were similar to those found at court. Virtually every city had a group of official city pipers whose court equivalent would have been the group of wind instrument players and trumpeters that followed the ruler and symbolized his authority. These instrumentalists could provide music for public ceremonies, perform signals and trumpet calls (for example, announcing the arrival of a herald or sounding a fire alarm) and play public concerts for the entertainment of the citizens. Members of these bands sometimes took up the function that would have been given to chamber musicians at a court and performed music on soft instruments, such as lutes, recorders, and viols.

Another musical group that was necessary was, of course, the church choir, and many independent cities spent a considerable amount of money to rival the church choirs supported by absolute rulers. Civic pride often demanded that the choir of the local cathedral be of the first rank, with music-making equal to that of any other city or court. In many of these cities, wealthy patrons contributed large sums of money for the expenditures of the cathedral, but often they could not do so openly. In fifteenth-century Florence, for example, the Medici family was instrumental in attracting musicians to the city and in paying them to grace the choir of the cathedral. Technically, though, these payments could not be made in an official manner. Florence was a republic, and the act of paying directly for the cathedral choir would have been seen by its citizens as an act of arrogance on the part of the Medicis, possibly as a step toward their usurpation of political power. Even though the Medicis were among the wealthiest families in all of Europe and ruled Florence from behind the scenes—something that everybody knew very well—they could not be seen as overstepping their boundaries in the matter of the choir.

One great advantage of many of these cities was that they tended to be important commercial centers where commerce was not, as at court, an activity considered improper for the nobility and better left to the commoners but the central activity of their citizens. In general, these cities tended to be more tolerant of political and religious dissent and that, coupled with the extensive commercial trading network they developed, encouraged the establishment of certain trades and professions. Printing and publishing, for example, thrived in these circumstances. Books could be published there that might have received much closer scrutiny from the Holy Office (the Inquisition) in places like Rome, and publishers had easier access to capital and know-how. As a result, many of these cities became major centers for the publication of music books and for the production of musical instruments. Their relative freedom and tolerance, together with their wealth, also attracted musicians from the surrounding areas and from places much farther away, creating a strong musical culture that followed a model unlike that of the courts. In one of the cities mentioned earlier, there was also a strong musical tradition of middle-class composition and performance. In Nuremberg, middle-class tradesmen and artisans formed groups of "mastersingers," later immortalized in the nineteenth century by Richard Wagner in his opera *The Mastersingers of Nuremberg*. Mastersingers, who were not professional musicians, were organized along the lines of the guilds that regulated the commercial activity of a city. Just as full membership in the guilds required a long apprenticeship, followed by a public exam that demonstrated mastery of one's trade, so the Mastersingers required a musical apprenticeship and an entrance exam at which the candidate would compose a new song according to strict written rules and answer some questions about the musical repertory. In addition, candidates had to prove that they were men of good character. At their monthly meetings, competitions would be held where the members were assigned a song to sing and were judged on their ability to sing it faithfully and according to the rules. Winners received small prizes and free refreshments, but, of course, the most important prize was the fact that they had triumphed over all other masters in a demanding competition. The tradition of the Mastersingers was extraordinarily long lived, and those belonging to the society felt they were carrying on a tradition dating from biblical times and, therefore, relied on unchanging written rules and avoided musical innovations. Thus, the music composed by these amateur composers is generally not of the highest quality, but the society they created and the evident pride (and civic pride) it generated were important to the sense of identity of the citizens of Nuremberg.

MUSIC AND RELIGION

Music had been an important part of religious service virtually from the very beginning of the Christian Church. In the period preceding Christianity, music and other arts such as dancing and acting had been an integral part of certain religious services and, in fact, even the birth of Greek tragedy was linked to religious celebrations. It is not surprising then that music was very much a presence in the church throughout the Renaissance, although the forms of this presence could vary considerably. In the sixteenth century, with the break of Reformed Churches from Rome, local musical practices could be rather different and in line with the prevailing religious ideology of a particular place. In the fifteenth and early sixteenth century, before the work of Luther, there was certainly a more unified situation in Europe. The fifteenth century is, in fact, the period when sacred polyphony became quite common in most important churches. Church choirs grew tremendously during this period, both in terms of number of choirs across Europe and number of choristers in each choir. Although it was not unusual to see only four or five singers of polyphony listed in the payroll of an important church at the beginning of the Renaissance, by the end of the same century the choir of a cathedral could easily number between twelve and sixteen singers, and some were even larger than that.

Before we talk about the role of polyphonic performances in church, though, we should remember that not all music heard in a church was elaborate polyphony. The official music of the Church, monophonic Gregorian chant, a repertory whose roots can be traced to the earlier Middle Ages before the invention of music notation, was heard in all churches of the period much more frequently than the relatively rare polyphony. A church-going individual in the fifteenth century could have spent most of his or her life going to church without hearing much polyphony, but he or she could not have gone even one Sunday without hearing some Gregorian chant. We should not think, then, that the increase in polyphony meant a huge increase in music in the service. Polyphony often replaced the simpler Gregorian chant but was not generally used for sections of the services that would not have originally used chant. Still, one could argue that, during the Renaissance, there was an increase in the complexity of the music used in all services. If we were to take a snapshot of the situation regarding church music around 1425 and around 1600, we would notice several major differences. By the year 1600, the relatively small choirs of

1425 had been replaced by large choral groups, often supported by instrumental ensembles of varying sizes and performing polyphony on a regular basis. Polyphonic compositions, which in 1425 were used sparingly and only in some of the more important churches, were now heard virtually everywhere, and smaller churches had the kind of choir that might have been found in a cathedral of the early Renaissance. Nevertheless, there were also points of similarity in the organization of these musical institutions.

Normally, choirs were run by a choirmaster, often known as *maestro di cappella* or *Kapellmeister*, whose responsibilities ranged from rehearsing the choir and choosing the music to providing basic instruction in music to the younger choirboys and, in some cases, advanced instruction to adult singers. Choirmasters were also expected to provide musical compositions according to the needs of the church, including music for weekly services and more elaborate pieces for special, unique celebrations. Often the choirmaster was the most famous of the singers of the choir, leading by authority and experience, and the highest paid among them. In theory, then, the choirmaster was supposed to be not only an accomplished composer, able to compose music that would be envied by the clergy of other churches, but also a teacher and an administrator of considerable skills. Because church choirs at important institutions were often composed of singers from different nationalities and with diverse backgrounds, the choirmaster sometimes had to keep the peace and make sure that nothing happened to disturb the church services. In addition, he had to deal with the administrators of the church or of the secular government, asking for the resources needed to do a satisfactory job. It should not surprise us that many of these choirmasters did not manage to fulfill all of these expectations. Some were good composers but poor administrators, some were unable to control the tempers of their singers, and some were good administrators but indifferent composers.

One function that the choirmaster did not have to fulfill was to conduct the choir like a modern conductor. The type of conducting that is done today, facing the choir with expressive gestures and movements, was unknown in the Renaissance. In many paintings and miniatures, when one of the singers seems to be in charge, we see him as part of the group standing at one end of the choir and lifting a hand unobtrusively to give the beat. The more emotional type of conducting to which we are accustomed for orchestras and choirs began to be practiced only in the nineteenth century and would have probably looked somewhat strange to Renaissance musicians.

The governing body of a cathedral would normally be the chapter of all the canons of a church. Canons (senior clergymen) occupied all the important positions within the hierarchy of that particular church and carried out the various administrative tasks necessary. The chapter elected a dean who was, for all practical purposes, the chief administrator of the church, especially since it was not uncommon in that period for bishops not to be in residence at the cathedral. Other canons were in charge of financial matters of the church school, of the necessary record keeping, and other similar matters. Some of the tasks were less glamorous; for example, one of the canons would usually supervise those employees entrusted with the task of keeping the church clean and chasing away stray dogs.

The official directly above the choirmaster was in charge of supervising the performance of all the liturgy, not just of polyphonic music, which was a relatively small part of the total. In many churches there would be short meetings between this official, often known as "master of ceremonies," and the choirmaster to review the musical needs of the church on a particular week or feast day. The choirmaster, having been told when music was needed, would then fetch the music books of the choir and select the appropriate compositions or, if needed, would sit down and compose a new piece. While we think of the act of musical composition as something that needs inspiration to succeed, an employer in the Renaissance normally assumed that a composer in his pay would compose on demand whatever music was needed at the time. Choirmasters could use the help of a junior choir member or one of the older choirboys, who would often be entrusted with the care of the music book and who copied the new music into the books of the church. Sometimes the singer in this position was also carrying out more delicate duties. Faced with the slow pace of composition by their beloved choirmaster Adrian Willaert, the *procuratori* (governors) of the church of St. Mark's in Venice voted in 1547 to double the salary of one of the young men of the choir, Baldissera Donato, with the condition that he would copy into the music books the new compositions of Willaert. The *procuratori* continued: "and since the above-mentioned master Adriano is a busy man, Baldissera will be expected to keep prodding master Adriano to compose that [music] in the name of the Most Illustrious Procuratori, and as soon as master Adriano will give him a new composition, he must copy it in the music books, and announce that to the Most Illustrious Procuratori, so that they can see what is being composed by master Adriano."[12] We can sympathize with the young Baldissera, who found

himself in the position of either having to be a nuisance to his immediate superior, the choirmaster Willaert who was by 1547 an older
and immensely respected figure, or face the disappointment of the
procuratori.

Another important member of the musical establishment of the
church was the organist, who was called upon to provide music with
or without the choir. A church organist had to be a consummate improviser, as most of the music he performed would not have been
written down in a score. Organists had to possess a tremendous
amount of musicianship, and it should come as no surprise that many
of them are among the best-known composers of the Renaissance.

A fair amount of music making also took place within the walls of
monasteries and convents. Although these institutions had lost some
of the prominent position they had enjoyed in the Middle Ages, many
of them had extensive land holdings and were quite powerful and able
to support in their churches musical establishments of the first rank.
The singing of nuns, as we have seen, was often praised in this period, and some convents were the destination of important visiting
dignitaries, who had heard accounts of their angelic singing.

CATHOLIC CHURCHES

Because music played an increasingly important role in Catholic
services throughout the Renaissance, it is hard to give a picture of a
typical workweek for a church choir that would apply equally well to
1425 and 1600. For one thing, it is likely that a fair amount of polyphony was heard not at the main weekly services but at special com-
memorative and votive services paid for by private citizens for the sake
of their souls or by associations (guild or confraternities) for the benefit of all their members. Also, descriptions of church services from
the Renaissance do not always give us much detail about the musical
performances. The chronicler of one of the most important events of
the fifteenth century, the dedication in 1436 of the newly completed
cathedral of Florence (topped by the marvel of engineering that is the
dome we can still admire today), was characteristically uninformative
when describing the mass of dedication attended by the Pope and his
choir. We are fairly certain that a composition by one of the most famous musicians of the period, Guillaume Dufay, was performed at this
service, as we have an elaborate motet by him with a text celebrating
the event and mentioning the Pope by name, but the narration of the

events does not mention this piece. Giannozzo Manetti, the writer, describes the music in this way:

> First there was a group of trumpeters, lutenists, and wind instruments, each of them carried a trumpet, lute, or wind instrument in his hands, and wore red clothing. In the meantime there was singing with so many and such various voices, and with so many harmonies carried even to heaven, that they seemed to the listeners as if they were angelic and divine songs, because they stimulatedthe listeners' ears with a wondrous sweetness of many voices that the listeners seemed stupefied as if they had been listening to the syrens' song of the legends. . . . But at the Elevation of the Most Sacred Host, all places in the basilica resounded with such harmonies, and with such concerts of so many various instruments that it seemed, not unreasonably as if the angelic and heavenly songs and sounds had been had been sent from heaven to us on Earth to whisper in our ears something unknowable, because of their unbelievable sweetness.[13]

Descriptions of more common services are often even less forthcoming, perhaps only mentioning that a Mass was sung and often not making a distinction between the singing of Gregorian chant and that of polyphonic pieces. Still, we can arrive at some conclusions regarding the use of polyphonic music in churches during the Renaissance. The composition of Masses became a major part of a church composer's duties, and polyphony in general became more in demand as the Renaissance progressed. We usually have much more surviving sacred music from late Renaissance composers than we do from those active in the earlier part of the period. It is true that, to some extent, the increased numbers are due to the introduction of music printing, which made it easier for works to be distributed and preserved.

At the celebration of a Mass, even one in the late Renaissance, there would be a mixture of polyphonic music, Gregorian chant, and reciting tones (a heightened way of reciting prayers). Some items of the Mass would have been traditionally heard in a reciting tone uttered by one of the priests celebrating the service. This was the case, for example, for the Gospel or the reading of the Epistle, whose text changed every day following the liturgical year. Other items would be traditionally heard in Gregorian chant. Here the performance might not be by the musical choir but by the assembled clergy of the church, since all priests were trained in Gregorian chant during their schooling. As we have seen, the text of many of these items also changed from day to day so that it was always appropriate to the particular celebration, and it was not interchangeable with that of some other day of the liturgical calendar.

Finally, there would be polyphony, which might include the whole Ordinary of the Mass, that is, the sections including those texts that do not change throughout the year, and perhaps some other motet at an appropriate point in the liturgy. The choir would be rather small, since not everyone on the payroll was present or singing at every service, and it could either sing from a pulpit (some churches designated one specifically for the choir) or stand somewhere in the vicinity of the altar. On special celebrations the choir might move to different locations in the church. In many churches it became customary to celebrate the Passion of Christ with the stations of the cross: The clergy and singers would process around the church, stopping at each station and singing sections of the Gospel text. Even more elaborate ceremonies could take place at important feasts. On Easter Sunday at some churches the clergy and singers would form a procession around the square in front of the church and reenact the Gospel narrative of the discovery of the empty tomb of Christ. A few singers would be hiding behind the closed doors of the church and eventually the procession would arrive at the doors, knocking loudly. The singers inside would then sing a short verse asking the crowd outside what were they seeking. The response would come: "We are looking for Jesus." Then the doors would be flung open while the singers sang "He is not here. He has risen," as they lead the procession to the altar and showed the faithful an open and empty tabernacle.

Aside from Masses and special celebrations, the singers were increasingly needed for the celebration of the canonical Hours, or Office. The Office consisted of a series of prayers and readings originally meant to organize the life of monastic communities around the idea of work and worship. In its strictest form, the Office required monks to rise in the middle of the night for a set of prayers, followed by silent meditation in the cloister and by another service around dawn. Such services continued regularly throughout the day. Outside monasteries these observances would have been impractical at best, but during the sixteenth century we can see an increase in the complexity of Vesper services (the evening services), which were widely performed for the laity throughout the year, and also of Nocturnes (night services), usually for Holy Week, the week before Easter. Several late sixteenth-century composers, for example, set to music the entire cycle of the texts for the Nocturnes of Holy Week, usually with rather emotional settings. Vespers were far more common in that they could be celebrated with polyphony on many feast days. On very important church holidays, in fact, the celebration really started with the Vespers on the eve of the feast day and concluded twenty-four hours later with the Vespers on the evening of the holiday. Singers on these occasions were occupied for at least three major services within a twenty-four-hour period.

Besides the regularly scheduled services of the church, singers could also be busy elsewhere. Many citizens would hire singers to mark an important occasion, such as a wedding, a funeral, or the ordination of a relative as a priest, nun, or monk. Also, a fairly important source of income and a chance to hear more polyphony came from Masses celebrated on behalf of the deceased. Often a will would direct the survivors to establish a permanent endowment at a church or chapel with the understanding that Masses would be said in perpetuity at designated intervals (such as once a year) on behalf of the soul of the testator. The payment could be barely sufficient to pay for a priest or large enough to have a full-fledged Mass with singers and polyphony. Those making their will would have the comfort to know that such services could possibly reduce their time in Purgatory, while for singers and priests this was a source of considerable additional income.

The most important change in the Catholic Church in this period was the so-called Catholic Reformation, or Counter-Reformation, which began with the convening of the Council of Trent. This council met intermittently between 1545 and 1563 and dealt with many pressing issues regarding not only religious dogma but also the training and behavior of priests, the reform of the liturgy, and so forth. In a climate so charged with doctrinal and political decisions, it is only natural that music would not receive a great deal of attention. Only at the very end of the last period of the council, between 1562 and 1563, in a series of sessions dealing, for example, with the reform of the Papal Curia and with the sacrament of communion, was music discussed at some length.

Since at least the seventeenth century, a legend circulated that the council was intent on prohibiting any use of polyphony during the service and that only the performance of a Mass by Palestrina (the so-called "Pope Marcellus Mass") saved polyphonic music from the ax. (We now know that this is very far from the truth and that there was never any serious consideration of a complete ban on church music.)

Several of the bishops with an interest in this matter had a long-standing interest in music reform, wanting to curb some of the excesses they had seen practiced by church choirs. In 1555, for example, Pope Marcellus II was described by his secretary as being upset at the joyful music sung by the papal choir for Good Friday, something he clearly felt to be inappropriate. Others complained of "licentiousness" in music meant for the divine service.

A committee appointed by the council for considering these matters arrived at a set of informal guidelines to be observed by all Catholic composers of sacred music. The most important is perhaps the injunction to write sacred music so that the polyphonic texture would not obscure the text being sung. There were also statements about the need to exclude any kind of secular music from the church and to write music that was reverent and pious. The amount of music composed for Catholic services not only did not diminish but increased in the decades after the council closed, and we can also detect an increase in the complexity and virtuosity of Catholic Church music at the beginning of the seventeenth century.

In conclusion, we can say that music of some complexity became fairly common during Catholic church services in the Renaissance. The effects of the Council of Trent were not to decrease the importance of music within Catholic worship, and we can safely say that its guidelines on music might have even been a stimulus to composers and musicians to increase the volume of music meant for religious worship. If around 1425 it might have been hard for a member of a congregation of a major cathedral to hear polyphonic music on a regular basis, by 1600 the same person could have had the opportunity to hear it several times a week.

MUSIC IN REFORMATION CHURCHES: MARTIN LUTHER

The religious appeal brought on by the religious reforms of the sixteenth century could not help but affect the status of music in the church. Reformers, such as Luther and Calvin, did not only hold opinions about matters of religious dogma that conflicted with those of the Catholic Church but also introduced changes in the liturgy that affected the role of music and the careers of church musicians. It would be a mistake to portray the Reformation as a monolithic bloc with consistent views on music. In reality, the positions of reformers on music varied considerably, depending on their own background and personal opinions. After its beginnings at the hands of Luther in 1517, the Reformation developed in different directions, from the Lutheran Reformation radiating from its center toward northern Germany and the East to the Calvinist brand of reform, particularly powerful in Geneva and to points west of Switzerland, and to the break from Rome of the Church of England. Martin Luther, the most influential of those reformers, was a passionate music lover who saw music as important and beneficial not only to religious services but also to human life in general. In the preface to an anthology of motets published in 1538, Luther described his feelings toward music:

> I would certainly like to praise music with all my heart as the excellent gift of God which it is and to commend it to everyone. But I am so overwhelmed by the diversity and magnitude of its virtue and benefits that I can find neither beginning nor end nor method for my discourse. [. . .] But when [musical] learning is added to all this, and artistic music, which corrects, develops, and refines the natural music, then at last it is possible to taste with wonder (yet not to comprehend) God's absolute and perfect wisdom in his wondrous work of music. [. . .] But any who remain unaffected [by polyphonic church music] are unmusical indeed and deserve to hear only a certain filth [dung] poet or the music of pigs.[14]

A musician who knew Luther, Johann Walther (d. 1570), left this description of the reformer's involvement with music: "Martin Luther took great pleasure both in plainsong and polyphonic music. I spent many hours singing with him and saw how happy and joyful he was then. He could never get enough of music, and he spoke about it magnificently."[15] Coherent with his praise and love of music, Luther set to involve his congregation more deeply in musical performance: "I also wish that we had as many songs as possible in the vernacular which the people could sing during Mass [. . .] for who doubts that originally all people sang these which now only the choir sings or responds to while the bishop is consecrating [the host]?"[16] Luther's first far-reaching reforms of the liturgy can be found in his *Deutsche Messe* ("German Mass") published in 1526. In it Luther argued for the continuation of Latin services but also stated that a German Mass should be introduced for the sake of the laity. These reforms were popular, and soon Lutheran Germany adopted a liturgy that effectively united Latin and German sections of the service. German hymns, known as

chorales, were introduced to allow the whole congregation to participate so that the doctrinal points and sentiments expressed in those
hymns could be understood by all and, with the help of music, help
the congregants to take the right path. While this approach dimin-
ished somewhat the importance of elaborate polyphonic music in the
service, it did not take any drastic steps toward eliminating choirs and
choral compositions. In addition it stimulated composers who adhered
to Lutheranism to provide new hymnals with the appropriate texts and
melodies in a tradition that reached its pinnacle in the works of Johann
Sebastian Bach in the first half of the eighteenth century.

Zwingli and Calvin

More radical religious reforms with important and negative effects
on music were proposed by Ulrich Zwingli and John Calvin in Switzerland. Zwingli, in particular, saw the correct path as one that purged
the church of all things that interfered with the worship of God. He
and his followers in Zurich began in 1524 a campaign to rid the
churches under their influence of all superfluous ornaments, destroy-
ing in the process religious vestments, books, relics, paintings, and
church organs. Zwingli took an uncompromising position regarding
music in the service, fearing that any use of music in the church would
be not only distracting for the congregation but also positively harm-
ful, as it kept them from concentrating on the word of God. Naturally, such views were simply catastrophic for composers and musicians
in areas controlled by Zwingli. Suddenly, they would find themselves
unable to earn their livelihood and without an outlet for their music.
The physical elimination of organs and music books was particularly
detrimental, as it destroyed a significant musical legacy for posterity.
Fortunately, although John Calvin was also extremely suspicious of
music, his position was less extreme. Calvin professed an appreciation
for the powers of music, but this appreciation also made him worry
about the power of music to spread ideas and behaviors that he found
unacceptable. These concerns were not new to the sixteenth century,
and, in fact, they were voiced very eloquently by the early Church
Fathers, for example, St. Augustine in the early period of the Christian Church. There was always a recognition that music's great power
could also lead to a loss of focus on the most important part of the
service and of one's life, the worship of God. In the preface to a book
of Psalms translated into French for the use of his faithful, Calvin
outlined his position:

Now, among all other things that are proper for recreation of human-kind, and for giving pleasure, music is either the first or among the most important, and we must deem it a gift from God made precisely for this purpose. For which reason we must be very careful not to abuse it at all, for fear of sullying it and contaminating it, and of converting it into our damnation, while it is meant for our benefit and salvation. Even if we had only this thought to consider, it would have to move us to limit the use of music, to make it serve all honest goals, and to make sure that it might never be the cause of wanton licentiousness, or of our becoming soft amongst immoderate pleasures, and [to ensure] that it might not be the instrument of buffoonery or of any shameless act. [. . .] And in fact we find by experience that it [music] has a secret and al-most incredible power to move our hearts one way or another. For which reason we must be the more diligent in regulating it in such a way that it be useful to us, and never detrimental.[17]

Calvin's prescriptions allowed some use of settings of Psalms in the church, although he wanted them to be set without polyphony and in melodies to be sung in unison. He did allow for simple polyphonic settings of Psalms to be used in private homes to provide entertain-ment without resorting to what he saw as lascivious and immoral love songs. Musicians in Geneva and other Calvinist cities faced a pretty clear choice: if they agreed with Calvin's reforms, they would assist in writing musical settings of Psalm texts for their congregations; if they did not, they had to move elsewhere to pursue their career. Choirs and musical establishments that had once been among the best in Europe were thus disbanded or severely reduced in sized, and strict limits were placed on musical composition. It is interesting to note how the opening of Luther's and Calvin's statements about music are very similar, but while Luther saw music's power as a gift from God to be enjoyed joyfully, Calvin came to a rather different conclusion.

THE REFORMATION IN ENGLAND

The effects of Henry VIII's break from Rome in 1533–1534 were slow to manifest themselves because of the peculiar character of the English Reformation. Although there were some among the English nobility and clergy who had differences of opinion with Rome, the major impulse toward the break from Rome was not so much ideo-logical as personal and political. Shortly after Luther began his reforms, in fact, Henry VIII had been dubbed "defender of the faith" by Pope Leo X in recognition of his strong opposition to Lutheranism. As a result, liturgical and theological reforms in England happened slowly and gradually, and were relatively tame when compared with those of the continental reformers. Over a period of almost twenty years, as the new Anglican service took shape, the role of music in English churches was reduced somewhat, and the texts set to music changed from Latin to English. Current guidelines also required that the polyphony be simple and that the text be set mostly syllabically, with "a plain and distinct note for every syllable one," as one set of instructions from 1548 reads. One very important change that followed the break of the Church of England was the closure of hundreds of monasteries and convents and many churches. These institutions had been essential in the development of music in England, and their demise meant that many good church choirs were dissolved and that some of the surviving religious institutions and choirs (among them the chapel of the king) gained in importance, concentrating significant musical activities in fewer locations.

In response to the changing demands, English composers began to set English texts to music in the style preferred by the Anglican Church, although Latin church music was still allowed in a few places. Gradually, forms such as the anthem (the equivalent to the Latin motet) became the center of the musical section of the services. Composers did not usually set Masses in polyphony, because that service was seen as hopelessly Catholic, but they developed music for Anglican services that could be rather elaborate and grandiose. In addition, some Catholics were allowed to worship in private, and they could have used music written for the Catholic service while worshiping in their homes. In the England of Queen Elizabeth, who reigned from 1558 to 1603, there was some tolerance for Catholics as long as they were not seen as threatening the monarchy and the Anglican Church. One of the most famous English composers of the time, William Byrd, remained a Catholic all his life and composed and published Catholic church music during the reign of Elizabeth. He was one of the favorite musicians of the queen, which might explain why he was allowed to continue to practice his religion undisturbed.

Anglican England, then, took a sort of middle ground between the more extreme instances of Protestantism and the practices of the Catholic Church with regard to music. Although there was definitely a reduction of opportunities for church musicians, all things considered, the musical life of England did not suffer dramatically, and we can note that the reign of Elizabeth brought an increase in the availability of secular vocal music and instrumental pieces.

MUSIC IN PUBLIC CEREMONIES

One important function of music throughout the ages has been to accompany public ceremonies and celebrations, whether of a political or religious nature or more closely tied to entertainments and diversion for the common people. Let us keep in mind, while we discuss these uses of music, that it is fairly normal for any type of public display to fulfill more than one function, with meanings and messages that might not always be apparent to us today without taking a closer look. For example, it is sometimes difficult to separate the political and religious aspects of such celebrations, because quite often a political event or a military victory would be solemnized by thanksgiving services for the saint on whose day that event fell. Thus, the decisive and unexpected victory of the European Christian powers against the Ottoman Turks in the naval battle at Lepanto, off the coast of Greece on October 7, 1571, was celebrated by some of the allies by elevating St. Justine's day, the date of the battle, to an important place among the feast days of the liturgical calendar. For years to come, the festivities apparently directed toward the cult of the saint would have also reminded the crowds and visiting dignitaries of a great victory and, thus, of the greatness of the state.

We are, of course, familiar with the power of music to move us to patriotic feelings or to feelings of solemnity, which is why we play patriotic songs, marches, and national anthems; why we sing our alma mater; or why we hear old standards such as the *Pomp and Circumstance* march by Elgar performed at so many school graduation ceremonies in the United States. It is not surprising, then, that music in the Renaissance could have been used to foster a civic spirit, the sense of identity of the population of a city or of a state.

In many European countries the Carnival season would bring the opportunity for public revelry. Perhaps nowhere in Europe was this celebrated as much as it was in the city of Florence in the fifteenth century. Florence, nominally a republic, was governed in that period by one of the most powerful families of the Renaissance, the Medicis, whose most visible member, Lorenzo, known as "the Magnificent," managed to control the government by placing his friends and allies in positions of power. The Medicis in general, and Lorenzo in particular, were great patrons of the arts and spent lavishly to attract artists, musicians, and writers to their court. Lorenzo himself kept a private correspondence with several artists (for example, the composer Guillaume Dufay) and took pleasure in writing verses and in musical pastimes. His general attitude toward life, and one that explains the importance given to the Carnival and *calendimaggio* (May Day) celebrations, can be summed up in the words of one of his poems: "How beautiful is youth, which is nevertheless fleeting. He who wants to be happy should do so now, for tomorrow is always uncertain." The Carnival culminated with Mardi Gras, a time of revelry before the Lenten penitential season, while the spring celebrations began on May 1 and continued in Florence until the feast of the patron saint of the city, St. John the Baptist, on June 24. During these times men and boys roamed the streets in *mascherate*, that is, in elaborate costumes, often in drag, singing simple songs full of jokes of a sexual nature and lewd double entendres. Under the rule of Lorenzo, parades with floats became increasingly common. On these floats, members of a guild or a particular neighborhood would provide simple staged scenes, accompanied by songs that described their profession in a humorous manner, or made fun of others. One of the surviving songs makes fun of the military band instrumentalists who were serving with the German mercenary armies with whom, unfortunately, Italians of the time were well acquainted: "We are Lanzi drummers, come from Germany with our drums and fifes where there is war and good wine. We have large flutes, thick, long and well bored; beautiful women, we can show them to you. . . ."

There could also be more serious displays, often known as *trionfi* (triumphs), with mythological or moralistic themes, which also contributed to the image of the city as a magnificent, festive place. All these celebrations contributed to the popularity of the Medicis who wanted to be seen as responsible for a "golden age" of happiness and good government in Florence. The reality might have been somewhat different, at least for the political rivals of Lorenzo, but there was definitely more than a grain of truth in that image. At the death of Lorenzo in 1492, Florence fell under the influence of the monk and preacher Girolamo Savonarola who succeeded in chasing the Medicis out of the city. He established a religious republic, with Christ as the ruler and himself as his earthly vicar. In short order Carnival songs and floats were replaced by simple songs with religious texts (the *lauda*, or "praise songs") and by bonfires of the vanities on which Florentines threw books, paintings, clothes, musical instruments, and also manuscripts of music. Savonarola did not discard the bawdy Carnival songs entirely but often reused the tunes, which must have been well-known to the population, writing new, devotional texts to fit them. One must wonder whether the newly pious Florentines ever thought of the original lascivious texts when they sang the old tunes.

The popularity of the lauda was not limited to Florence, but these simple songs, usually written in uncomplicated homophonic texture, could be heard throughout the Italian peninsula, and similar pieces were written in other countries for the same reason. Confraternities that had roots in late medieval penitential fervor could be found virtually everywhere. The lay members of these confraternities met regularly, and one of the activities would be the communal singing of devotional songs for a variety of occasions: from celebration of a saint's day to a member's funeral. This singing was often public, as it took place in processions that were at the center of the religious life of cities. Some of the more dedicated confraternities were those of the so-called flagellants, those who would take part in a procession whipping themselves to atone for the world's sins and to ask for mercy. Occasions such as these could effectively mobilize an entire city or town in ways that have become somewhat alien to us. It is sufficient to visit one of the smaller European cities where these traditions have survived to notice the excitement and the single-minded concentration of the population on the event. Often tourists are more tolerated than welcome at these celebrations, but the impetus is definitely one tied to dynamics internal to the city and to motivations that resonate with the local inhabitants.

Religious and political processions were also quite plentiful. Some cities, such as Venice, were so fond of different types of processions that activities of this type occurred, on a large or small scale, virtually every few days throughout the year. In Venice some of the processions were very solemn and involved the entire government, visiting ambassadors, the guilds and confraternities of the city, and the majority of the population, either as participants or spectators. The doge (duke), the elected ruler for life of the Republic of Venice, would leave his palace several times a year to visit one of the many churches of the city, usually in commemoration of some important event in the history of Venice. The most splendid of these occasions was without a doubt the annual ceremony known as the "wedding to the sea" that took place every year on the day of the feast of the Ascension. The custom had started as a visible reminder of the Republic's naval might and of its far-flung maritime empire in the eastern Mediterranean. The doge and the rest of the government would leave the palace and embark on the state barge, the so-called "Bucintoro," a boat resplendent with gilded ornaments and crimson cloth. Followed by a flotilla of ships and boats, with the singers of the chapel of St. Mark's singing motets in the Bucintoro, the naval procession moved to the opening of the port where they disembarked to hear Mass at a local church. After that, they would proceed farther toward the open sea, and the doge would fling a golden ring into the ocean, pronouncing the ritual words: "We marry thee, as a sign of true and eternal dominion." Having performed this ceremony, the cortege would return to St. Mark's while the singers sang "something joyful." Although the religious element was present and on center stage, there is no question that all those present would have been bursting with civic pride totally unrelated to religious feelings and that one of the goals of this exercise was to impress upon friends and foes alike the magnificence of the Republic.

Finally, one more use of music was more subversive: music could be used to display political or religious dissent and even to introduce improper sentiments in a particular context. The abbess of a convent once complained to the authorities because a local priest was making advances to one of her nuns. He would come to sing in their church and would sing pieces with texts from the Song of Songs, some of the most sensual passages in the Bible, making sure that the nun in question would understand his misuse of a sacred text. In one example, the abbess cites a motet dedicated to the Virgin Mary, which began "How fair art thou" and concluded with the words "and I languish because of my love," which the priest sang while making eyes at the young nun and added: "and he cannot sing well, and all the nuns are laughing and it's a great scandal."

In another instance, a couple of young patricians were stopped by the police during Carnival for singing an obscene parody of the sacred litanies often sung during religious processions. Music and poetry criticizing the government or a particular political figure could be easily made up and, in effect, contained a political message of dissent.

GUILDS AND CONFRATERNITIES

An important factor in the life and the artistic environment of many cities of the Renaissance was the presence of well-organized confraternities and guilds. Confraternities were organizations of laymen who gathered to share the cult of a particular saint and also performed acts of mercy and charity. Guilds were usually professional organizations uniting all the workers in a particular trade. Guilds often took a particular saint as their patron, but their main role was not religious. In many cities membership in a guild gave an individual a legal and social status within the city and allowed him to participate in political life. In addition they provided financial help for their members when they were sick or disabled, offered low-cost housing, paid for the dowry of a member's daughter when he could not afford it, paid a pension to the aged, and even provided a place for burial in the communal tomb they usually held in a local church.

In Renaissance London the members of the twelve major guilds were allowed to wear a distinctive livery, and the masters of these guilds elected the most important city officials. In medieval and Renaissance Florence, belonging to the guilds was essential, and no one could be elected to a public office without a guild membership. Even noblemen could not hold office without having been accepted into one of the guilds. Guilds and confraternities participated in public processions and ceremonies, often with violent arguments among themselves to claim a particularly prestigious place in the proceedings. Even in places where the guilds did not hold as much political power, the local ruler would often protect and encourage their activities, which provided an outlet for the middle and lower classes to participate in the public life of the city without actually holding much real power. In many European cities guilds and confraternities were actively engaged in the patronage of the arts. The combined resources of an organization could do what the single member could not afford to do, that is, pay for expensive art works or for the staging of elaborate celebrations. In the Netherlands, for example, confraternities dedicated to the cult of the Virgin Mary played a major role in the development of polyphonic sacred music in the Renaissance. The most famous of these, the Confraternity of Our Lady in Antwerp, had daily services that included organ playing and singing of sacred music. This example is not isolated, and we know of many cases where music was commissioned by confraternities and guilds, usually for the celebration of their patron saint's day.

Musicians employed by the guilds and confraternities were usually not full-time employees of those organizations; in fact, it was not uncommon for the warden of a guild to contract with the singers of the local cathedral to come sing for a celebration sponsored by his guild. In many cities this enhanced the income of the musicians, who profited from the competition among guilds and confraternities. So much money was spent by some confraternities on these activities that often local governments would be forced to remind them of their original charitable mission. When the great composer Claudio Monteverdi turned down an offer to rejoin the court of Mantua, from which he had been fired a few years earlier, he responded by praising his working environment in Venice. Monteverdi first noted that he was being paid 400 ducats a year for his work as director of music at the ducal church of St. Mark's, an enormous sum at a time when a very nice house could be rented for fifty ducats a year. Then he added:

> And this is the first particular, as regards basic income: then there is occasional income, which consists of whatever extra I can easily earn outside St. Mark's, of about 200 ducats a year (invited as I am again and again by the wardens of the confraternities) because whoever can engage the director [of St. Mark's] to look after their music—not to mention the payment of 30 ducats, and even 40, and up to 50 for two Vespers and a mass—does not fail to take him on, and they also thank [the director] afterwards with well-chosen words.[18]

The quality of the music and of the performance at these events was undoubtedly very high. An English traveler, Thomas Coryat, visited Italy in 1608 and left a description of a celebration at one of the main confraternities of Venice that included elaborate music:

> This feast consisted principally of Musicke, which was both vocall and instrumentall, so good, so delectable, so rare, so admirable, so super excellent, that it did even ravish and stupifie all those strangers that never heard the like. But how others were affected with it I know not; for mine owne part I can say this, that I was for a time even rapt up with Saint Paul into the third heaven.[19]

Even discounting for some hyperbole, it is obvious that concerts of this sort achieved the desired effect, that is, to show all "those strangers that never heard the like" the magnificence of one's city. Coryat tells us that the ensemble playing consisted of about twenty singers and twenty-four instrumentalists; this would have meant employment for a sizable percentage of the best musicians of the city, for whom, in many cases, any payment would have been in addition to a regular salary from a less occasional job.

As we have seen, one other way in which guilds and confraternities contributed to the musical life of a city was by fostering the singing of simple pieces in the vernacular language. Many of these organizations had rules concerning the appropriate place for such singing, whether as part of devotional services, of funerals for their members, or of special celebrations. Quite often the singers of these simpler pieces were not the skilled singers of more complex polyphony but amateurs, often members of the confraternity itself.

MUSIC IN SECULAR ACADEMIES

Music was also cultivated in private or semiprivate gatherings known as academies. Academies could vary from very informal get-togethers, where several friends united by a common interest would share an occasional evening, to highly formalized groups with statutes and strict rules and regulations for the behavior of their members. The success of the academies (by the mid-1500s there were more than 200 academies in Italy alone) was due to the revival of Greek culture fostered by Renaissance humanism. There were academies dedicated to the study of the sciences, of literature and poetry, of philosophy, and so forth, and even some that were dedicated entirely to music. As the century progressed, more music academies were founded, some devoting themselves to the cultivation of one particular branch of music. One of these, the Accademia Filarmonica in Verona, Italy, has the distinction of having the longest history of any musical academy. Founded in 1547, this academy still exists today, including its music library that houses volumes originally bought by the academy for its members in the sixteenth century. Similar academies were founded in other European countries, one of the most famous being the Académie de Poésie et de Musique, founded in 1570 by Jean Antoine de Baïf and Joachim Thibault de Courville in Paris. Typically, the activities of a music academy might include debates about musical matters, instruction in music provided by the musicians hired with the funds collected from the members, and, in some cases, even concerts that might be open to the public. Academies were very influential in the development of music in the sixteenth century, especially by providing a forum for theoretical debates. Not all debates produced lasting results: The "archicembalo" of Nicola Vicentino, a harpsichord with six keyboards and the ability to split an octave into as many as thirty-one notes (instead of the usual twelve), was too impractical to be successful, but many of the discussions about words and music, for example, deeply influenced music in the late sixteenth and early seventeenth century. One of the most famous and influential informal academies was the so-called Camerata de' Bardi, a musical salon hosted by Count Giovanni de' Bardi in Florence. Its members included noblemen and professional musicians—among them Vincenzo Galilei, a lutenist and theorist, and father of the scientist Galileo Galilei—and its meetings resulted in a new musical aesthetics that held solo singing with accompaniment in a new "recitative" style as the most appropriate way to set texts to music. The discussions of the Camerata set the stage for the birth of opera at the turn of the century.

Excerpts from the Statutes of the Académie de Poésie et de Musique (Paris, 1570)

The list of rules established for this academy shows a high degree of organization. The founders of the academy wished to restrict the circulation of the music written for the gathering, so that this repertory could be heard only there. Strange as it might seem, this is one of the few documents that actually establishes a rehearsal schedule for a musical group (normally documents are silent about this detail). Notice also the very modern attitude toward the division between audience and musicians, with clear rules as to the behavior of the public.

> *Neither the musicians nor the listeners will in any activities of the Academy contravene the public laws of this Realm.*
>
> *The musicians will be required to sing and recite the measured words and music for two hours every Sunday, according to an order established among them, for the privilege of the listeners registered in the book of the Academy.*
>
> *All the musicians will be required, unless they give a reasonable excuse, to come to the meeting room each day at an appointed time to rehearse the music each of them will have studied separately, which will have been distributed by the two Founders of the Academy, whom the musicians will be obliged to follow and obey in musical matters.*
>
> *The musicians will swear not to give out any copy of the songs of the Academy to anyone without the consent of the whole Company.*
>
> *Should one of the musicians fall ill, he will be cared for and treated solicitously until he recovers fully.*
>
> *A medallion will be struck carrying an emblem agreed upon by the members of the Academy, which the listeners will wear to gain entry. If one of the listeners should pass from this life to the next, the heirs of the deceased will be required to return the medallion to the Academy.*
>
> *During the singing the listeners will not talk or make noise; they will remain as quiet as they can until the song being performed is finished. While*

a song is being sung neither will they knock on the doors of the room, which will be opened at the end of each song to admit listeners.

If a member, after having heard one or two concerts of the Academy, requests a refund of the money he has advanced, it will be returned to him.

No listener will touch or pass the barrier setting off the stage, and no one other than the musicians will enter there. Neither anyone will handle the book or the instruments, but, remaining off the stage, they will treat with respect everything that honors and serves the Academy, whether it be its book or its personnel.

Whoever breaks any of the above laws, whether musician or listener, will be excluded from the Academy and no longer allowed to enter there and will forfeit any monies paid, except when, after the transgression has been repaired, the members of the Academy consent and agree otherwise. (Signed Baïf and Thibault)[19]

MUSIC IN RENAISSANCE UNIVERSITIES

Music studies at many of the major universities of the Middle Ages and early Renaissance had been usually restricted to the study of very abstract theoretical questions, mostly dealing with the relationship of music and mathematics as evidenced in the mathematical relationships that govern musical intervals. It was also permissible to consider philosophical or cosmological questions that involved music, but more practical studies were seen as beneath the dignity of a university. This frame of mind was a consequence of the attitudes toward music expressed by philosophers from Greek Antiquity to the early Middle Ages. The Greek philosopher Aristotle (384–322 B.C.) considered practical instruction in music desirable only in educating the young so that later in life they could become "good judges of musical performances," but he felt very strongly about those who pursued music as a profession: "We may accordingly reject any professional system of instruction. . . . On such a system a player makes [music] serve the pleasure—and that a vulgar pleasure—of the audience to which he is playing. That is why we regard his performance as something improper in a freeman, and more befitting a hireling."[21]

The late Roman philosopher Boethius (d. A.D. 525?) placed the study of music within the liberal arts. He echoed Aristotle when he classified musicians into three categories: performers, composers, and critics:

But those of the class which is dependent on instruments and who spend their entire effort there—such as kitharists [that is, players of a particular string instrument] and those who prove their skill on the organ and other musical instruments—are excluded from comprehension of musical knowledge, since, as was said they act as slaves. None of them makes use of reason; rather, they are totally lacking in thought.

The second class of those practicing music is that of poets [that is, composers], a class led to song not so much by thought and reason as by a certain natural instinct. For this reason this class, too, is separated from music.

The third class is that which acquires an ability for judging, so that it can weigh rhythms and melodies and the composition as a whole. This class, since it is totally grounded in reason and thought, will rightly be esteemed as musical. That person is a musician who exhibits the faculty of forming judgments according to speculation and reason relative and appropriate to music concerning modes and rhythms, the genera of songs, consonances, and all the things which are to be explained subsequently, as well as concerning the songs of the poets.[22]

Boethius also placed the "music of the spheres," that inaudible music produced by the motion of the heavens, as far superior to actual earthly music. These attitudes shaped the role of music in medieval learning. Although already in the late medieval period some scholars were beginning to question Boethius's views on music, favoring a more practical approach, the world of the universities tended to be relatively conservative in this respect.

In the Renaissance, some universities, especially those in Italy and Germany, began to teach music from a more practical point of view. Influential lecturers on music were active in cities with major universities but had somewhat loose ties to the institutions without a formal appointment. Many of those who wrote books on music theory in this period were also practical musicians, conducting choirs and performing regularly, and it is obvious that we see here a renewed interest in practical music as a legitimate field of study. Some writers even seem to reject the need for a rigorous course of theoretical study altogether. The Flemish composer Adrianus Petit Coclico (d. 1562) described in a book the teaching methods of the great Josquin Desprez, whom he claimed, perhaps not entirely truthfully, as his own teacher: "My teacher Josquin Desprez never rehearsed or wrote out any musical exercises, yet in a short time made perfect musicians, since he did not hold his students back with lengthy and frivolous instructions."[23] Coclico here might have simply been trying to legitimize his own teaching method by attributing it to a greater master, but it is interesting that his definition of musician is very different from that of Boethius. Now it's not the judge or critic to be held in highest esteem but the practical musician and composer, who does not need extensive knowledge of theoretical and philosophical arguments about music. This new attitude can be seen, of course, not just in music, but in the sciences in general, which begin to explore empiricism to a degree not seen earlier in Western Europe.

MUSIC IN PRIVATE HOMES

One of the most difficult contexts to study is that of the private home. Contrary to what happened for churches and courts, the records of private households of the middle and lower classes are not likely to have survived and, in many cases, might not have been very informative anyway. It is also relatively difficult to make general statements that would cover a period of almost two centuries in different countries and cities, and in households belonging to different socioeconomic classes. One generalization that is possible is that, during this period, art music became more accessible to the middle classes. The factors for this include the invention of music printing, which changed dramatically the musical landscape of Europe; the wider availability of cheaper instruments, especially the lute; and the fashion that made the middle classes take up aristocratic pastimes, such as music.

On one end of the spectrum we could place aristocratic homes, where music making was certainly somewhat elaborate but did not always involve a resident group of musicians as a court would. In the wealthiest of these homes special celebrations would be marked by the hiring of musicians to play and sing. We have scattered evidence that shows wealthy aristocrats gathering some of the best musicians of their city in their home for a musical soirée. In some cases, according to the polite behavior of the day, there might not have been a straight exchange of money for performance but a more subtle relationship in which the patron would bestow "gifts" on the musicians, and the musicians might also benefit from the good will of an important patron. More regular music making might have been confined to the members of the family, helped by a few musicians, one or more of whom would be also teaching music. The fact that in the sixteenth century we find musicians who describe their main occupation as being that of free-lance music teacher means that there must have been a growing market for private individual instruction, just as the social

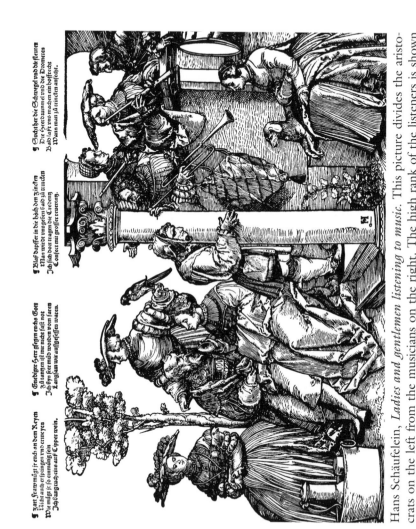

Hans Schäufelein, *Ladies and gentlemen listening to music*. This picture divides the aristocrats on the left from the musicians on the right. The high rank of the listeners is shown by the clothes they wear, and by the presence of a hunting falcon on the wrist of the standing gentleman. (Courtesy of Foto Marburg, Art Resource, New York.)

code of the period demanded a higher degree of proficiency in music from those who wanted to appear sophisticated and fashionable.

It is somewhat difficult to be specific about activities that have left no trace and would not have been memorable enough to deserve a special description. Some information can be taken from inventories of households taken after the death of an individual. It is apparent that in the sixteenth century, private ownership of musical instruments, especially keyboard instruments and lutes, was becoming more common. It is a little harder to know what would have been the size of a typical private collection of printed music, because notaries taking inventories had an annoying habit of lumping together books in descriptions such as "a small box with books" or "fifty books of different types." Occasionally, an item in an inventory stands out for its musical connections. A 1560 inventory of a private household lists "a table with eight sides, with a chest attached underneath, with its key, and eight little stools to hold the music books for playing," which is a piece of furniture with a specific musical use, a type of table that is familiar to modern scholars from some Renaissance paintings. Performers could sit around this table, each with his or her music stand, and play ensemble music in a perfect setting. A delightful picture of the type of music making that could have taken place in a private home is contained in the opening section of one of the most famous music manuals of the Renaissance, *A Plain and Easy Introduction to Practical Music,* published by the Englishman Thomas Morley in 1597. As usual, in the case of such manuals, the book is written in dialogue form, and the opening sees a student asking for help from a music teacher to learn this desirable social skill. The student, Philomathes, describes a dinner in a private home where a discussion about music began and continued with heated arguments on both sides. Here is how Philomathes describes his predicament:

> But he still sticking in his opinion, the two gentlemen requested me to examine his reasons and confute them; but I refusing and pretending ignorance, the whole company condemned me of discourtesy, being fully persuaded that I had been as skillful in that art [i.e., music] as they took me to be learned in others. But supper being ended and music books (according to custom) being brought to the table, the mistress of the house presented me with a part earnestly requesting me to sing; but when, after many excuses, I protested unfeignedly that I could not, every one began to wonder; yea, some whispered to

others demanding how I was brought up, so that upon shame of mine ignorance I go now to seek out mine old friend Master Gnorimus, to make myself his scholar.[24]

Notice that bringing out of music books after supper and singing by the guests are described here as "according to custom," not as unusual or strange in any way. Another portrait of the kind of informal music making described above can be found in the *Dialogue About Music,* published in 1544 by Antonfrancesco Doni. Doni imagines that a group of his musician friends has gathered together for discussions about music and performances of selected pieces and provides a narrative in dialogue form of their debates plus scores of the compositions sung. Here is how the dialogue goes before the singing of the first piece:

> GRULLONE: I want that the first piece we sing be a madrigal composed in praise, and let us sing it in honor of Candida.
>
> OSTE: Beautiful music and divine text! Who wrote the music?
>
> GRULLONE: Claudio Veggio [a minor composer].
>
> MICHELE: Then it can only be perfect. Let us try it.
>
> BARGO: Grullone, you take the bass; Michele, take the alto, and Oste will take the soprano.[25]

This scene rings true, as it depicts not a formalized, rehearsed music performance but a sight-reading of pieces in which vocal parts are assigned on the spot, in the way that so troubled Philomathes in the earlier excerpt. The preface to Doni's work illustrates why information on these informal gatherings is so hard to come by. In dedicating the work to Marquis Malvicino, Doni writes: "The music that is performed in the house of Your Excellency with lutes, keyboard instruments, wind instruments, flutes, and voices, and the music performed in the house of the honored gentleman Alessandro Colombo is most worthy, and the consort of viols heard in the house of Sir Guido dalla Porta is admirable."[26] If it were not for brief passages such as this, sometimes we would have absolutely no knowledge of the kind of music making that took place in homes like those of the three gentlemen in question. As it is, this quote only whets our appetite, but provides very little evidence beyond confirming that high quality music making took place in private homes.

MUSIC IN THE THEATER

One of the venues where one could hear music making in the Renaissance was the theater. The term "theater" could indicate a variety of situations, from the elaborate court presentations we have discussed earlier to much more common fare. In the sixteenth century, especially, staged plays were often presented outside of the court setting. Itinerant or semi-itinerant groups of actors toured from town to town with a stock repertory that might have included both written plays and simple plot lines to be filled in with improvisation. This last type of theatrical performance is often called "commedia dell'arte," an Italian term that means, more or less, "professional comedy" that is staged by professionals and not by amateurs. Music in these entertainments would have a place in a few situations. First, there could be music outside the play but as part of the entertainment, that is, before the beginning of the play and between the acts. Second, there could be music at appropriate places in the play, for example, when a character is singing a serenade or a love song, or if dancing is mentioned. Many plays of the period, from Italian Renaissance plays to the works of Shakespeare, abound in situations where music is necessary. Actors were trained to sing so there was no need to engage additional singers, but often a company might need to hire one or two instrumentalists to accompany the singing on stage. Some of the pieces meant to be sung during staged plays do survive, but in semi-improvised comedy these did not need to be written down so a large part of this repertory is lost. In general, in "commedia dell'arte" and other similar traditions, the script, a little more than a guide to the performance, would indicate to the actors what type of scene was to be performed but left to the actor's knowledge of the stock characters the actual lines to be said. Similarly, it would indicate a comic scene with physical humor only as "they horse around" and the need for a song with indications such as "then he sings" without indicating what song was to be sung.

The function of music within this context would have been no different from that in a modern movie or the incidental music still found in many plays.

A Contract between a Company of Actors and a Lute Player
Contracts of this type were often finalized with a handshake and not committed to paper. The fact that this contract was drawn might be due to

the prospect of touring abroad or perhaps to some previous problems between the two parties. The fine of twenty-five ducats would have been a sizable incentive to honor the terms of the contract.

January 9, 1559

Mr. Zuanbattista from Verona, lute player, son of Francesco de Cavrinis, on one side and Mr. Marin the Frenchman, the comedy or skit actor, son of the late Mr. Zuan Papiglian from Le Mans, in Brittany, on the other side, stipulate with this document that they have formed a society, to last for one year from today. Mr. Zuanbattista promises, throughout the said year, with all his effort and art, not holding back when confronted with toil or danger, either here in Venice or in any other land wherever it will be needed, to play the lute in every occasion when Mr. Marin, his kids, and the others in the company will work, and perform their skits, comedies, or Moorish dances, as is appropriate for a good and honest partner. And for his part Mr. Marin promises that in any place where he will perform these skits, comedies, or Moorish dances of his, he will give every day to Mr. Zuanbattista the eighth part of all the daily profits, whether he is healthy or sick, without any fraud or deception. And if one of the partners fails the other on the above-mentioned terms, he will be forced to pay 25 ducats, with the understanding that each of them can be arrested and thrown in jail in any country or place for violating those terms. And they asked me, the notary named below, to write this public legal document in the vernacular, as they prefer, and to give one copy of this to each of them.

[Witnesses:] Mr. Melchior Coressi, tailor, from the parish of S. Moisè, and the Reverend Hieronimo Vinicio, doctor in canon law and canon of the church of St. Mark's in Venice.[27]

CONCLUSIONS

The various examples of music making presented in this chapter are not meant to be comprehensive. In fact, in order to be anywhere near comprehensive in treating such a huge subject (if such a thing were possible), one would need to write a much larger book than the present one. It is not important, however, to know all the various manifestations of music in Renaissance society as much as it is to be aware of the great variety of ways in which music appeared in that society. It is easy to look at a society in a place and time so far away and see only the surface, which creates an illusion of uniformity. The preceding discussion has demonstrated that, on the contrary, the musical landscape of the Renaissance was as vital and vibrant as our

own, although certainly in different ways. Today we benefit, or perhaps suffer, from the abundance of recorded and broadcast music,
which makes the musical experience one that is never too far away from
our ears. This does not mean that the squares, streets, homes, and
palaces of Renaissance cities were not filled with music. As a sixteenth-
century visitor to the city of Antwerp, the Italian Ludovico
Guicciardini, remarked: "one can see at almost every hour of the day,
weddings, dancing, and musical groups . . . there is hardly a corner of
the streets not filled with the joyous sound of instrumental music and
singing."[28] This is the image we should have of the musical life of a
Renaissance city.

NOTES

1. Thoinot Arbeau, *Orchesography,* transl. by Mary Stewart Evans, with
a new introduction and notes by Julia Sutton (New York: Dover, 1967), 12.

2. For a lively and interesting look at some of these cults, see Carlo
Ginzburg, *The Night Battles: Witchcraft and Agrarian Cults in the Sixteenth
and Seventeenth Centuries,* translated by John and Anne Tedeschi (Baltimore,
Md.: Johns Hopkins University Press, 1983).

3. William Prizer, "North Italian Courts," in Iain Fenlon, ed., *The Renaissance* (Englewood Cliffs, N.J.: Prentice Hall, 1989), 136.

4. Quoted and translated in Tess Knighton, "The Spanish Court of
Ferdinand and Isabella," in Iain Fenlon, ed., *The Renaissance* (Englewood
Cliffs, N.J.: Prentice Hall, 1989), 344.

5. Quoted and translated in Anthony Newcomb, *The Madrigal at
Ferrara, 1579–1597,* 2 vols. (Princeton, N.J.: Princeton University Press,
1980), vol. 1, 24.

6. Castiglione, *The Courtier,* 108–9.

7. My translation from Marin Sanudo, *I diarii,* ed. R. Fulin et al. (Venice:
Visentini, 1879–1903), vol. 16, cols. 206–7.

8. My translation from Jeanne Marix, *Histoire de la musique et des
musiciens de la cour de Bourgogne sous le règne de Philippe le Bon (1420–1467)*
(Strasbourg: Heinz, 1939; reprinted. Genève: Minkoff Reprint, 1972), 38–
9.

9. Quoted in Claudio Gallico, *L'età dell'Umanesimo e del Rinascimento*
(Turin: EDT, 1978), 138–41. Author translation.

10. Walter L. Woodfill, *Musicians in English Society, from Elizabeth to
Charles I* (New York: Da Capo Press, 1969), 137.

11. Quoted in Craig Monson, "Elizabethan London," in Iain Fenlon, ed.,
The Renaissance (Englewood Cliffs, N.J.: Prentice Hall, 1989), 319.

12. The documents can be found in my Ph.D. dissertation, *The Chapel of St. Mark's Under Adrian Willaert* (Ph.D. diss.: University of North Carolina at Chapel Hill, 1986), 333.

13. Quoted in Guillaume Dufay, *Opera omnia*, ed. H. Besseler (Rome: American Institute of Musicology), 1948), vol. 1, pt. 2, xxvii. Author translation.

14. Martin Luther, *Works*, vol. 53, ed. by Ulrich S. Leupold (Philadelphia: Fortress Press, 1965), 321–2.

15. Piero Weiss and Richard Taruskin, *Music in the Western World* (New York: Schirmer Books, 1984), 104.

16. Luther, *Works*, vol. 53, 36.

17. Jean Calvin, Preface to *Psaumes octantetrois de David, mis en rime par Clèment Marot et Théodore de Beze* (Geneva, 1551; facs. ed., New Brunswick, N.J.: Friends of the Rutgers University Libraries, 1973), no pagination given. Author translation.

18. Claudio Monteverdi, *The Letters*, rev. ed., ed. by D. Stevens (Oxford: Clarendon Press, 1995), 191.

19. Quoted in Jonathan Glixon, *Honoring God and the City: Music at The Venetian Confraternities, 1260–1807* (Oxford: Oxford University Press, 2003), 157.

20. Quoted and translated in *The Renaissance*, ed. by Gary Tomlinson, in *Source Readings in Music History*, Oliver Strunk, ed., vol. 3, rev. ed. (New York: W. W. Norton, 1998), 62–63.

21. Aristotle, *The Politics*, translated, with an introduction, notes and appendixes by Ernest Barker (Oxford: Clarendon Press, 1946), 348.

22. Anicius Manlius Severinus Boethius, *The Fundamentals of Music*, translated, with an introduction and notes by Calvin M. Bower, ed. by Claude Palisca (New Haven, Conn.: Yale University Press, 1989), 51.

23. Weiss and Taruskin, *Music in the Western World*, 100.

24. Thomas Morley, *A Plain and Easy Introduction to Practical Music*, ed. by R. Alec Harman (New York: W.W. Norton, 1973), 9.

25. Antonfrancesco Doni, *Dialogo della musica*, ed. by G. Francesco Malipiero (Vienna: Universal Edition, 1965), 8–9. Author translation.

26. Doni, *Dialogo*, 5.

27. Unpublished document in the Archivio di Stato di Venezia.

28. Quoted and translated in Kristine K. Forney, "16th-Century Antwerp," in Iain Fenlon, ed., *The Renaissance* (Englewood Cliffs, N.J.: Prentice Hall, 1989), 361.

CHAPTER 5

Musical Instruments

As we have seen earlier, the Renaissance was a pivotal period for the history of instrumental music, with more instrumental music surviving from the sixteenth century than from all previous centuries combined. This was also a period when instrument makers modified old instruments or invented new ones and when new playing techniques were applied to older instruments. The evidence we have comes from a wide variety of sources: paintings and drawings often showed musical scenes; manuals were published to help the amateur gain musical proficiency, often giving us basic information about the playing technique and the structure of the instruments; and treatises were written attempting to classify the whole field and to provide as complete as possible a picture of the available instruments. In addition, we have a fair number of Renaissance instruments surviving in museums around the world. None of these sources should be taken without some careful consideration, as they all have some pitfalls and problems. For example, a painting could show an instrumental ensemble not likely to exist in real life. Often this is the case for religious paintings showing angels playing harps, lutes, and trumpets together, when we know from other sources that trumpets were usually not played together with quieter instruments. Obviously the artist in these cases was simply painting instruments that he thought appropriate for a group of angels, without regard for musical accuracy. A Renaissance book about musical instruments might aim for completeness without discriminating between instruments that might have been extremely rare and those commonly used in everyday performances. Symbolic associations also played an important role. Trumpets were symbols of power and were shown accompanying a ruler entering a subject city; lutes became symbols of gentility and good breeding, and a portrait genre of the sixteenth century shows a demure young lady playing a lute. Variations of this (some were adapted to serve as portraits of saints) were plentiful and show us that, for a socially respectable family, it might have been important to portray daughters of marriageable age as being prim, proper, and in possession of social graces, among which the ability to perform on a musical instrument was considered very important. Even the instrument collections now found in museums can be misleading, as they often include an abnormally high number of very elaborate instruments, probably preserved through the centuries because of their status as artistic objects rather than for a practical purpose.

The general public's view of Renaissance instrumental music often identifies the recorder as the most popular instrument of the period. Although there is some truth in this view, the real picture is much more interesting and complex, with different types of instruments sharing the stage. Renaissance instruments were often divided into families, with members of the family spanning the range from high to low. For example, recorders could be made in sizes ranging from a tiny recorder sounding an octave higher than the standard soprano recorder to a great bass recorder sounding an octave lower than a regular bass. Instrument makers often made instruments in "consorts," that is, matching groups covering a wide range of pitches and meant to be played together. At a time when there was not a commonly accepted pitch standard (as today with A = 440 Hz), this ensured primarily that there would not be a problem of intonation among the members of a group. The fact that the same maker made a group of instruments at the same time also meant that these instruments matched in tone color so that, in ensemble playing, there would be a homogeneous sound quality in the group. Some of the surviving consorts also display interesting details of construction, such as the type of decoration, inlaid motifs, or other defining features, which show that the instruments were meant not only to be played but, in a sense, also to be shown together.

One type of group that the Renaissance lacked altogether is anything approaching the modern orchestra. That is, there was no name available that would indicate a fairly large standard combination of instruments in the way that saying the word "orchestra" makes us think of a group composed of violins, viola, cellos, double basses, and assorted wind, brass, and percussion instruments. Furthermore, much instrumental music was meant to be played as chamber music with one player to a part. There was no universally accepted standard instrumental combination, and, in fact, the vogue for a particular type of ensemble or for a particular instrument might be limited to a geographical region. In England, for example, a type of chamber group mixing particular string and wind instruments was fairly common. Relatively large ensembles were not common and were usually found at important celebrations, court festivities, and other similar occasions, but no scores approaching the complexity of later orchestral scores were ever composed in this period.

The most complete source for information on Renaissance instruments was actually published a few years after the accepted ending date of the period. Between 1614 and 1620 the German composer Michael Praetorius published a monumental work in three volumes, the *Syntagma musicum*, with a large section dedicated to musical instruments including illustrations that showed all the instruments known to him. His illustrations are arranged by families so that, for example, one page shows a complete family of recorders, one presents all the sizes of flutes, and so forth. On the other hand, we know from various types of evidence that it was possible to have a mixed or "broken" consort, that is, a group made up of instruments from different families. Here the guiding principles would be to respect the main subdivisions of instruments found in the late Middle Ages and Renaissance, that is, between "high" (loud) and "low" (soft) instruments, so that an instrument meant primarily for outdoor performances with a loud, strong tone would not be paired with quieter instruments, such as lutes, harps, flutes, or recorders. Very few Renaissance ensemble pieces include any indication of instrumentation, and the few that do are often somewhat flexible in their suggestions.

Modern performers of Renaissance music do not use instruments manufactured during the Renaissance. Most of the surviving instruments are not in perfect playing shape and certainly could not stand the wear and tear of normal playing. There are exceptions, of course, but most of the instruments heard in modern performances are modern copies of older instruments made on the basis of close study of museum instruments or with the aid of the indications included in Renaissance treatises. We can be fairly sure that most of these instruments reproduce the sound made by their original counterparts many centuries ago, but, of course, we cannot be absolutely positive.

It is impossible within the scope of this book, to give a complete picture of the variety of instruments available during the Renaissance. It seems that the increase in importance of instrumental music was paralleled by a great increase in the types of musical instruments available. The following discussion, although it might seem rather exhaustive, is in fact not at all complete, but it can serve to give a flavor of the instrumental music of the period. With this in mind, let us look at the most popular instruments in the various families.

KEYBOARD INSTRUMENTS

Among keyboard instruments, the two most important in this period are the harpsichord and the organ. The organ had been around for centuries and its basic principles did not change in the Renaissance. It consisted (as it does now) of a keyboard controlling the flow of air to a set of tuned pipes. The sound of the organ (registration) could be changed, but, in general, such changes did not occur very frequently. When set, the timbre remained the same throughout a piece. Organs, even church organs, were smaller than those we usually see in modern churches, with fewer pipes and smaller keyboards. Usually only one keyboard (called "manual") was provided, not the multiple manuals we see on modern organs. Besides church organs, Renaissance musicians also played smaller organs known as positive and portative organs. The positive organ ("positif") was a chamber organ small enough to be transported with relative ease and placed on a table or a stand for a performance. Even smaller was the portative organ, which was used in the Middle Ages and through the early Renaissance. This instrument was small enough that a player would balance it on his lap, playing the small keyboard with one hand while pumping the bellows with the other. Just like modern accordions and concertinas, Renaissance organs needed a steady supply of air at a predetermined pressure. Churches employed not only organists but also men whose only job was to pump the bellows (made of leather and wood) that supplied the air to the organ. In a charming fifteenth-century print of an organist and his wife we see the organist playing a positive organ in his house while his wife is happy to pump the bellows. The organ is a positif placed on a table, without pedals and with a limited range of pipes. The presence in the background of the picture of the marital bed and of the dog at the feet of his masters signify that this is a married couple.

Israel van Meckenem, *The organist and his wife*. (Courtesy of Foto Marburg, Art Resource, New York.)

Churches and courts spent a sizeable amount of money to keep these instruments in good playing condition. Mice and rats often chewed on the bellows and other leather parts, thieves sometimes stole the pipes to sell the metal, and parts did wear out. Organ makers tended to be among the most specialized of instrument makers. They usually dealt primarily in organ making and, just as organ makers today, had to spend a great deal of time on location, building, and installing organs for churches within a certain geographical area. Virtually no church organs survive from the Renaissance in the original state. When it was time for a new instrument or new music demanded new technical innovations, the existing organ would be scrapped or, in some cases, modified to suit the new demands, for example, by adding more keys or pipes.

A particular type of organ was the regal, or reed, organ, an instrument whose sound is still with us in modern church organs, which are often fitted with an organ stop originally meant to imitate the regal. The regal had a characteristic buzzing sound, and it was sometimes used when a special effect was needed.

The harpsichord was the counterpart of the organ in the secular sphere. A Renaissance harpsichord would have only one keyboard (a manual) with a range quite a bit smaller than that of a modern concert piano. The biggest difference between a harpsichord and a piano is in the way the sound is produced. While the strings of the piano are struck by small hammers, the strings of a harpsichord are plucked by a small plectrum. Because the player could not effectively control the force with which the pick plucked the string, he or she had much less control over volume and expression than is available on a piano. Harpsichords were built entirely of wood, and many surviving models have very elaborate and beautiful paintings on their lids. Renaissance harpsichords tended to be lighter and smaller than the instruments available to Baroque composers, such as the ones known to Bach or Handel. Instrument makers and theorists experimented with the design of the harpsichord resulting, for example, in a harpsichord with vertical strings in the manner of an upright piano and in harpsichords built to try out theoretical notions about the subdivision of the octave.

There were several smaller subtypes of harpsichord, such as the spinet and the virginal, popular in Elizabethan England and said to be a favorite instrument of Queen Elizabeth herself. A visitor to the royal palace, Thomas Platter, commented in 1599: "We saw in addition many more costly virginals, instruments [i.e., keyboard instruments], positive organs, and organs of which Her Royal Majesty is a great lover and connoisseur. And amongst others we were shown an instrument or virginal whose strings were of pure gold and silver, and they said the queen often played this very charmingly."[1]

Harpsichords could be used as solo instruments or to accompany a soloist, and Renaissance paintings often show harpsichords in mixed ensembles of voices and instruments or instruments alone.

BOWED STRING INSTRUMENTS

The family of bowed strings was extremely important both for professionals and amateurs. The most important subfamily in this group, however, was not that of the violin but the viola da gamba (also known as viol or, simply, gamba). Violins were played in the Renaissance, but their use was often reserved for dance music, not for the more elaborate ensemble pieces. The violin begins its rise to prominence only at the beginning of the Baroque period in the early seventeenth century, and by the late 1600s it had replaced the viola da gamba as the most important bowed string instrument. Viols have several points of similarities with the violin family but also important differences in construction and playing technique. The most important differences are the use of six strings instead of the four strings of the violin, the frets on the fingerboard just like a modern guitar, the shape of the holes cut in the soundboard (usually the so-called C holes, not the F holes of the violin), and the overall construction of their bodies. Viols are heavier than violins and have a different shape: sloped shoulders and a flat back. The playing position and technique resemble that of a violoncello in that viols (even those that are relatively small) are held between one's legs, with one important difference in the position of the hand on the bow: While in a modern cello the palm of the bowing hand faces downward, in a viol it faces upward. The bow is also lighter than that of a violin. The combination of construction, frets, lighter bow, and different playing technique give a viol a light, silvery tone that is perfect for blending with others in consort playing. Viols ranged from treble viols for the upper parts to bass viols and later to larger basses known as violone ("large viol"). The violone lives on in the double bass of the modern orchestra, which borrows some of its characteristics from the earlier instrument. Also, some schools of double bass playing still favor the "underhand" (palm upward) bowing position typical of viols.

Viols were considered instruments fit not only for professional but also for aristocratic amateurs. In his *Book of the Courtier*, Castiglione mentions viols as appropriate instruments for the cultivated amateur and describes the music of a consort of four viols as "most suave and exquisite." Larger viols could be played as solo instruments, and a whole repertory is available for versions such as the English lyra viol, played in such a way that the performer could strike chords as well as a melody in the manner of the later solo sonatas for cello and violin by Johann Sebastian Bach. The viol has the distinction of being one of the first instruments whose playing technique was discussed in a printed treatise, the *Regola rubertina,* by the Venetian instrumentalist Silvestro Ganassi, a member of the official band of the Venetian Republic.

One bowed string instrument not often mentioned in the modern literature, but extremely important in the musical landscape of the Renaissance, is the so-called lira da braccio. This instrument, which looked roughly like an oversized violin and was played in the same position, probably evolved from the medieval fiddle. Its most distinguishing features were a very flat bridge so that its strings lay on a relatively flat plane. The performer could easily play chords with his or her bow, drawing it across more than one string at a time in a way that is much more difficult on a modern violin. The lira da braccio also sports strings laying outside the fingerboard to be used as "drones." This instrument often appears in drawing and paintings representing Orpheus or other figures from Greek mythology. It was the instrument of choice of the improvisers active at the Italian courts of the Renaissance and, as such, it was considered a noble instrument. Unfortunately, the tradition of using the lira da braccio for accompanying improvisatory performances means that we have virtually no music written specifically for the instrument, since these pieces were not usually written down. The little we have seems to point to a playing technique that resulted primarily in a succession of chord patterns that provided a simple accompaniment for the improvisations of the soloist.

Although not as important as the viol, the violin did make its first appearance in the Renaissance, likely as the result of modifications made to the earlier medieval fiddle. The first documented record of the violin comes from frescoes painted by a minor painter in the northern Italian cities of Bergamo and Saronno around 1535. The first musical composition asking specifically for a "violino" was published by the Venetian composer Giovanni Gabrieli in 1597, but the range

Michael Praetorius, from *Symtagma musicum*. This illustration shows three different sizes of viola da gamba at the bottom, a viola bastarda (a type of viola da gamba) at the top, and a lira da braccio, the favorite instrument of improvisers, in the center. (Courtesy of Bärenreiter-Verlag, Kassel.)

of the part suggests that it was probably written for an instrument closer to the size of a modern viola, and, in fact, the terminology regarding violins (and other instruments, for that matter) was at times vague throughout this period. It is interesting to note that only a few years before the publication of this piece the first professional violinist was hired at the ducal church of St. Mark's in Venice where Gabrieli was organist. The virtuoso Francesco da Mosto was given the task of playing with the instrumental groups as well as the choir of the church, "since"—as the 1581 document says—"he was heard with such satisfaction by all when he played with the organ on Christmas night."[2] The shape of a late sixteenth-century violin would be immediately recognizable by a modern public, although its sound might be unfamiliar to many in today's audiences. Compared with our modern violins, the Renaissance violin used strings made of animal gut, which give a warmer sound than the metal strings of modern violins but lack their edge and carrying power. The fingerboard and neck were positioned at a different angle in relation to the body. The more pronounced angle of the neck of modern violins, introduced to counteract the tremendous forces exerted on the instrument by modern metal strings, was unnecessary since gut strings could not be tightened nearly as much. The bow was lighter and the shape of the bow stick was closer to an arc rather than the convex shape of modern bows.

Finally, several paintings of dance bands including violins often show a playing position that is closer to that of a modern country fiddler, that is, with the violin braced against one's chest, not under the chin as it is played in classical music. The solo history of the violin really begins only with the works of several early seventeenth-century Italian composers, for example, Biagio Marini (ca. 1587–1663), who cultivated solo and ensemble sonatas for the violin and introduced techniques such as the playing of double stops (i.e., more than one string at a time) that have remained staples of violinist techniques. The ascendance of the violin was so sudden that by 1636–1637 the French theorist Marin Mersenne could call it "the king of instruments."

PLUCKED STRING INSTRUMENTS

Plucked string instruments were extremely popular in the Renaissance. Instruments of the lute family were made in large numbers and cheaply, and thus were available to a rather large section of the population. Lutes have a pear-shaped body made of thin strips of wood and a short neck with a fingerboard with frets (in the manner of a modern guitar) with six gut strings. Several sizes of lutes were available. The whole instrument is actually quite light in weight, and its sound is rather soft. Because of its light construction and the type of strings used, the sound of a lute string fades rapidly once the string is struck and is not as resonant or sustained as that of a modern guitar. One way to give more power to the lute was to outfit it not with single strings but with courses, that is, pairs of strings tuned at the same pitch or an octave apart. In the sixteenth century it was common for five of the six strings of the lute to be doubled in this manner.

The history of the lute reaches back into antiquity. Instruments that seem to be similar to the Western European lute can be found as far back as approximately 2000 B.C. in Mesopotamia and somewhat later in Egypt. It is likely that the lute was introduced to Europe by the Arabs in the thirteenth century, probably through Spain, and, in fact, even its European name is derived from its original Arab name, el-'ud.

The single most important reason for the popularity of the lute was a change in playing technique that occurred during the Renaissance. Before that period, lutes were usually played as melody instruments, and paintings invariably show the performer holding a quill in his or her hand and using that as a plectrum. The right hand is shown in such a position, almost lower than the strings, that it is unlikely it would have been used in a strumming motion; rather, it would have been played one string at the time as a melody instrument. Toward the end of the fifteenth century we notice a change as performers stop using a plectrum and change their hand position to resemble more that of a modern classical guitarist. Theorists of the period talk about the new possibilities of "joining high and low notes," and performers began to use this new technique to make the lute a self-sufficient instrument. From that time on the lute could be used not only in consort with other instruments but also as a solo instrument and to accompany a solo voice. The new technical possibilities opened by this change made the lute an important instrument in the development of solo instrumental music in the Renaissance. Composers and publishers also fed the public's appetite for lute music by arranging vocal music for the lute so that virtually all the famous vocal pieces of the sixteenth century could be found in a lute arrangement. Instrument makers took advantage of this new situation by producing cheaper lutes, together with expensive ones made of precious woods, or even ivory, and decorated with elaborate inlays. Late sixteenth-century inventories of lute-making shops show that these were organized along quasi-industrial lines, with stocks on hand totaling several hundred lutes and with developed networks for exporting those instruments to locations all over Europe. In a short period of time the lute became an instrument found in all musically educated households.

Toward the end of the sixteenth century, lutes sometimes received extra strings, particularly if they were to be used for accompanying singers. Early seventeenth-century instruments, going by names such as theorbo, archlute, and chitarrone, had an extension of their neck in order to place several additional bass strings of much greater length than those usually found. Such strings were tuned before the performance and could not be fingered by the player, but their value was in the added depth and foundation they provided, turning the lute into one of the preferred accompaniment instruments of the period.

While the lute was popular all over Europe, in the Iberian peninsula its place was held by a closely related instrument, the vihuela. The body of the vihuela looks like that of a small guitar but with less pronounced curves. The instrument is strung like a lute and its construction is somewhat lighter than that of a modern guitar. In the Renaissance, the guitar, also popular in Spain, was usually strung with four strings, not six as was the case for lutes and vihuelas. In Renaissance Spain, the distinction between guitar and vihuela was one of repertory and social status, perhaps more than one of construction. The guitar was a popular instrument, while vihuelas were played by virtuoso soloists and by members of the aristocracy. The repertory of the vihuela is quite large, as several Spanish composers ("vihuelistas") published a number of books combining the features of a teaching manual and an anthology. The pieces there range from simple pieces, obviously chosen for their pedagogical value, to more elaborate solo pieces and arrangements of vocal music.

Guitars in the Renaissance moved from the popular sphere to the highest court circles. From its Spanish origins, the guitar was imported to Italy, primarily through the kingdom of Naples then ruled by a Spanish dynasty. In late sixteenth-century Italy, the guitar had a great success not only as a novelty but also because of the increased interest in accompanied solo singing. Guitars, which were often strummed rather than plucked in the manner of a lute, provided a wonderful way of accompanying some of the dance songs found at court entertainments. The popularity of the guitar increased in the early seventeenth century, especially since guitar music was notated in a simplified system known as "alfabeto" (alphabet), similar to that still used by those who want to learn basic accompaniment patterns on the modern guitar.

One other string instrument was used in the manner of the guitar (that is, strummed) and prized more for its rhythmic contribution than for the performance of solo music. The cittern, very popular in the

British Isles, has a round body, quite flat (about as thick as that of an electric guitar), is strung with metal strings and played with a plectrum. Citterns were usually played in consort with other instruments in England. Some of the surviving Renaissance citterns are extremely elaborate, not only with inlays but also with figures carved in the neck and on the back of the body.

BRASS INSTRUMENTS

We have seen earlier that there were definite restrictions on the use of brass instruments by gentlemen and ladies. Brass instruments were traditionally instruments played by professionals, and their use was originally confined to a few situations, in part because of the technical limitations of some of the instruments. Throughout this period trumpets were "natural" trumpets, that is, built of long sections of tubing without any valves that would have enabled them to play a chromatic scale, and, thus, generally limited to the pitches we associate with bugle calls. Trumpets of this type are usually depicted accompanying royalty or members of the ruling class. They took part in processions and other similar occasions where they represented a symbol of authority, and they were used to signal the announcements of official heralds on public squares. Naturally, trumpets also accompanied rulers and generals on the battlefield where their role was eminently practical, as they were called upon to play the signal needed for an orderly functioning of the army. Ships, especially those engaged in military duty, usually required the presence of at least one trumpeter for the same purpose. The trumpet was ubiquitous in paintings of the period, but aside from being shown accompanying secular authorities, its most frequent appearance is as an instrument played by angels. Such depictions have more a symbolic value than a true historical value and should not be taken as indications that the use of the trumpet was widespread in sacred contexts. A mid-sixteenth-century description of a church ceremony held to ask for divine help for a departing general who was, of course, accompanied by his trumpets and drums, bemoans the fact that at one point during the ceremony the trumpeters were unable to restrain themselves and began to play, drowning out the words of the celebrant.

Most of the surviving trumpets from this period have two small rings soldered to their body: one close to the mouthpiece and one to the bell. These rings, as is clear from paintings and drawings, were used to hang small standards bearing the coat of arms of the ruler. Trumpets were also different from the modern trumpet in the size and shape of the bell and mouthpiece, and in other elements of construction. They could also be made in different sizes so that there could be an entire musical group made up of trumpets. Players often specialized in one particular range and type of instrument.

The brass instrument most often shown in paintings and miniatures of the early Renaissance is a strange hybrid that we call a slide trumpet. This instrument is often shown as part of a three-member dance band in which the two upper parts were taken by a shawm (a type of wind instrument we will discuss shortly) and the lower part by a slide trumpet. The principle of the slide trumpet is similar to that of the trombone. The difference is that, in a slide trumpet, only the mouthpiece and a length of tubing connected to it are stationary, whereas the whole body of the trumpet slides. The player of the slide trumpet could produce more pitches than are available on a natural trumpet by sliding the body of the instrument in and out, thus shortening and lengthening the total length of the tube in the manner of the slide of a trombone. The instrument is usually shown as having an S-shaped body, and its length and weight would have made it somewhat unwieldy. It is unlikely that it would have been suitable for fast musical passages. From what we know of fifteenth-century dance music, though, the lower part tended to be slow moving and not particularly complicated, and for this type of musical performance the slide trumpet would have been acceptable.

By the end of the fifteenth century the slide trumpet had been virtually replaced by the trombone, an amazingly ingenious development. The name "trombone" is Italian for "large trumpet," but in the Renaissance the instrument was generally known in England and France as "sackbut," a term we still apply to replicas of early trombones to distinguish them from our modern instrument. The testament to the success of the trombone is the simple fact that its design is virtually unchanged since that period. Modern trombones sport a larger bell and somewhat thinner tubing due to technological advances in metallurgy. The slightly different construction of Renaissance trombones gave them a more mellow sound, which blended well with voices. Because of this characteristic, one of the main uses of the trombone in the late sixteenth century was to accompany and support the voices of a church choir. Trombones were made in various sizes, that is alto, tenor (the most common), bass, and contrabass. Larger instruments had a pivoting handle attached to the slide, which enabled the performer to reach the fullest extension of the slide.

One more instrument should be mentioned in this category even though it consists of a mixture of features from the brass and woodwind families. In the music of the late sixteenth century, trombones are often grouped with an instrument called cornetto (also known by its German name, Zink). The cornetto (plural, cornetti) was usually made of wood. A curved piece of wood would be split lengthwise, hollowed out, then glued back together and wrapped in leather (which helped seal the two halves of the instrument). Finger holes would be made, similar to those of a recorder, but the instrument was fitted with a small removable mouthpiece resembling that of a trumpet, except for its smaller size. Thus a performer would use his lips as he would in playing a trumpet but moved his fingers as if playing the recorder. In contemporary paintings cornetto players are often seen playing not from the center of their mouth but a little to the side. Because of the small size of the mouthpiece, this was often a preferred position, so that one's lips could fit the very small, almond-shaped mouthpiece. Cornetti can be distinguished by the gentle curve of the instrument and by the dark color, due to their leather covering. Most cornetti shown are of the curved type, but there was also a type with a straight bore in which the mouthpiece and the instrument were carved together from one straight piece of wood. This was often called a "cornetto muto" (mute cornetto), and in contemporary illustrations it is easy to confuse it with a recorder. Cornetti also came in a variety of sizes, including a low-pitch variety called "serpent," from the characteristic shape of its body. Although the cornetto fell out of favor in the early seventeenth century, being replaced by the violin in most sacred music, serpents continued to be used, particularly in England, for church choirs and military bands well into the nineteenth century. The cornetto was prized in its heyday as being the instrument closest to the human voice, with a high degree of agility and the ability to use dynamics and expression just like the voice. It was often used to support the upper parts of a choir as well as for playing independent instrumental parts.

WOODWIND INSTRUMENTS

The woodwind family probably comprises the largest variety of types and sizes of any other instrument family of the Renaissance. The most familiar to us is without a doubt the recorder. It is true that recorders were quite common in the Renaissance, but the Renaissance player had at his or her disposal a great range of wind instruments. Some were played both by cultivated amateurs and by professionals, others were usually reserved for professionals alone. Recorders and flutes were the wind instruments most acceptable for an amateur from the upper section of society. This is obvious not only from the number of paintings showing aristocrats playing or holding flutes or recorders but also by the fact that recorder playing is the subject of perhaps the earliest detailed musical manual of the Renaissance, the *Fontegara* of Silvestro Ganassi, published in 1535. The publication of such a manual would have been unnecessary if the instrument had been limited to professional musicians, since these individuals usually learned their craft directly from a teacher. The fact that this manual was published means that there was a sufficiently large public interested in recorder playing but not able to take frequent lessons with a professional.

Recorders came in a variety of sizes, perhaps more than any other wind instrument. The soprano and alto were encountered most frequently, although tenors and basses were also used to make up a complete consort. The construction of a Renaissance recorder varied slightly from more modern examples. The differences are relatively subtle, but they must have produced a sound that was softer and less reedy than that of a later recorder. From the kind of musical examples found in the *Fontegara* we can see that the playing technique was quite advanced and that a good player must have been expected to attain a very high level of proficiency.

Renaissance flutes are also immediately recognizable to a modern musician, but the Renaissance flute was a much simpler instrument than the one played in modern symphony orchestras. It was essentially a piece of wood with a cylindrical bore and simple finger holes. It lacked the elaborate mechanism necessary on a modern flute to play a fully chromatic scale, and its tone was much softer and less penetrating than that of a modern metal flute. It was also made in a variety of sizes, roughly speaking from alto to bass. There is little doubt that, at least until the late seventeenth century, it was the recorder that was favored of the two instruments, so much so that it was often designated simply as "flute." The flute, on the other hand, was often called "German" flute, or transverse flute (because of the way it is held by the player). Both recorders and flutes were used mostly for secular chamber music, although flutes or fifes were occasionally seen in bands accompanying the procession of a ruler in the manner of more recent fife and drum corps.

Another small type of recorder was extremely popular in the Renaissance. In illustration after illustration we see a long, thin recorder played with only one hand, while on the same wrist is hanging a small drum, which the musician is beating with a stick on his free hand. This combination is the so-called pipe and tabor, the one-man dance band of the Renaissance. By beating the characteristic cadence of a dance and playing a simple tune with the three-holed pipe, a single musician could provide everything that was needed for a dance. This combination was in use in England until the beginning of the twentieth century and still survives in areas of France and Spain.

Many wind instruments of the Renaissance fall into the category of double-reeds, similar to modern oboes and bassoon. The most popular was the shawm, which was identified by a variety of names throughout Europe. A shawm is very similar to an oboe, but, due to its larger bore and size and to its playing technique, it is a much louder instrument. Instruments very similar to shawms are still used in folk music in many countries around the world, from the shepherd's pipes heard until recently at Christmas time in Italian cities to Middle Eastern and Eastern instruments. A shawm was not a delicate instrument: Its loud, nasal voice was used both in dance bands, making up the core of the three-person band standard in fifteenth-century dancing, and in religious and political processions. The series of prints known as "The Triumph of Maximilian I," commissioned by the Emperor Maximilian to impress others with the splendor of his court, shows a horse-mounted military band made up of shawms and trombones (see p. 60). The players all have cases hanging from the saddle where the instruments could be placed while traveling.

Shawms were usually made of one piece of wood and came in several sizes, although the larger among them were rather unwieldy. The smaller shawms had only plain finger holes without keys, in the manner of a recorder, but in the larger sizes the lower finger holes were usually covered by simple keys, because the player's hand could not have stretched far enough to cover them. The double reed was much wider than that of a modern oboe. The player did not pinch the reed as much as is done on a modern oboe, and these factors contributed to the loudness of the instrument. The shawm takes a fairly high amount of pressure on a player's lips and cheeks, and it was often fitted with a device called a "pirouette," a wooden disk around the reed where the player could rest his lips, thus tiring less easily. When looking at many contemporary paintings, it is easy to mistake a shawm for an instrument with a trumpet-like mouthpiece because of the way a pirouette looks when being played. The shawm retained its popularity throughout the Renaissance and eventually gave way to its offspring, the oboe. It is worth noting that the English term "oboe" derives from the French "hautbois" ("loud, high-pitched woodwind"), originally employed both in France and in England to designate the shawm.

A double-reed instrument more familiar to us is the curtal, the predecessor of the bassoon. This instrument was also known by a variety of other names, among them Dulzian in Germany, fagotto in Italy, and basson in France. Aside from the near lack of keys, a Renaissance curtal looks just like a modern bassoon, although its tone is a little louder and coarser. Curtals were sometimes fitted not with a bell but with a cap looking a little like a salt shaker. This served to muffle its sound somewhat, making it more suitable for a mixed consort of instruments. We know that curtals were occasionally used in churches as support for choirs or with other instruments. Although many sizes were made, the most widely used was the one equivalent to our modern bassoon. Smaller and larger sizes were available but not in use throughout Europe.

An instrument similar to the curtal that has not left any traces in the modern orchestra is the so-called racket. The curtal, just like the bassoon, is built by boring a piece of wood with two parallel bores joined at the bottom, thus creating a tube twice as long as the apparent length of the instrument. A racket, on the other hand, was usually made by taking a piece of wood or ivory and boring nine channels up and down the block. By connecting these channels to form a continuous tube, the makers created an instrument sounding much lower than expected for its apparent size. All rackets sounded in the low range, even those that were made in smaller sizes. The soprano racket was a little less than five inches long, but the nine channels drilled into its body gave its bore an actual length of almost forty-five inches. In addition, its thin, cylindrical bore and the fact that the end of the bore was stopped made the racket sound an octave lower than normal for its bore length. The instrument makers showed their ingenuity by the way they drilled a number of oblique channels into the body of the instruments to make all finger holes within reach of the player. The racket had a limited range, and it usually had twelve finger holes, requiring the player to use the middle joint of the first fingers to cover a couple of those holes. Although the instrument had a value as a support for the bass, its limited range and expressive ability caused it to lose popularity in the seventeenth century. An elaborate set of metal rackets is found, still in its original case, in a Viennese museum. The tubing is covered by metal bodies shaped in the form of dragon heads. The instruments are still in playing condition and it is reported that when they are played, the tongues in the mouths of the dragons vibrate.

Medieval and Renaissance instrument makers created a class of double-reed instruments based on a small but important change to their playing technique. Instead of letting the player take the double reed between his lips, the makers protected the reed with a cup-shaped cover, leaving the player to blow in a slot cut in the top of the instrument. A whole category of instruments, which we call capped double reeds, was made using this simple device. The most popular of these is probably the crumhorn, a piece of wood curved in a characteristic hook shape and named after the Old English term for "crooked horn." Crumhorns had a very narrow bore and a limited range. Their buzzy and nasal tone sounds strange to modern ears, but crumhorns were quite popular in the period. The relatively soft volume made it possible to pair crumhorns with a variety of other chamber instruments, and, as usual, they were made in different sizes so as to be able to form an independent consort. Not all capped double reeds were soft, though. The Rauschpfeife was a capped counterpart of the shawm and, as such, was used in virtually all places where a shawm could be played, especially in outdoor groups. It was particularly cultivated in German lands. Other similar instruments appeared in the late sixteenth and early seventeenth century but most had relatively limited diffusion and did not reach the same height of popularity.

We should not leave the woodwinds without mention of one of the most ubiquitous instruments, the bagpipe. Although not usually employed in "art" music, bagpipes were often shown in paintings, either to create an idyllic pastoral atmosphere or to show musical entertainments of the peasants. In a famous painting by Bruegel, a single bagpiper plays while peasants dance with an abundance of high kicking steps, different from those of most of the dignified dances of the nobility.

PERCUSSION INSTRUMENTS

When we look at the percussion instruments of the Renaissance we notice an interesting situation. From discussions of music and from the visual arts we know that many different types of percussion instruments existed in that period, but we have no indication in scores of how and when such instruments would be used. Only a few dance treatises give us some basic percussion patterns but without much additional explanation, if any. We know that percussion instruments were not used in sacred music, and we know that they were probably quite common in dancing. It is also very likely that certain secular pieces, the more rhythmic and popular ones, could have been performed with some type of percussion accompaniment. Another very widespread use of percussion instruments was as military or processional instruments. Drums were used by all armies, and their use was sometimes extended to ceremonies involving a military leader. In a print showing the funeral procession for Emperor Charles V, we see a musical group made up of drummers and trumpeters, each with the coat of arms of the dead emperor hanging from the instrument. Each drummer carries two drums in the shape of modern orchestral tympani but much smaller. Similarly, in the "Triumph of Maximilian I" mentioned earlier, drummers are part of the musical groups shown. Instruments available ranged from the military drums to triangles to tambourines and more unusual percussion combinations, for example, the so-called Rommelpot (Rumble-pot). This was a folk instrument made by closing an earthenware pot with an animal skin and placing a stick in a hole through the skin. By moving the stick up and down, or rotating it, a sound is produced that can be used to provide a rhythmic accompaniment. In modern-day fast food restaurants one can hear miniature versions of the Rommelpot every time someone moves a straw through the plastic lid of a soft drink cup.

This list of instruments is, of course, rather incomplete. There were many other instruments, some with a more regional diffusion and use and others for which there is virtually no surviving written music. One example will be sufficient: the hurdy-gurdy was quite popular in the Renaissance. This instrument looks like a large oblong box, containing a number of strings similar to those of a violin. The player turns a crank which moves a wheel inside the instrument: this wheel acts like a violin bow by rubbing the strings and causing them to produce a sound. Some strings are always in contact with the wheel and function as drones. A melody can be played over this accompaniment by pushing keys or buttons placed on one side of the instrument. Each time one of these is pushed, a string is pressed against the moving wheel. From being an instrument used in art music in the Middle Ages, the hurdy-gurdy gradually became associated with folk music and often with the music played by beggars in the streets of Renaissance cities. City dwellers in the Renaissance were no doubt familiar with its sound but, because it was not used for the music preferred by the educated classes, it has left no tangible mark of its presence in the period, although it is still with us as a folk instruments in many national traditions.

THE MUSICAL INSTRUMENT TRADE

Throughout this chapter we have described and discussed various types of musical instruments but have given little attention to a whole branch of the musical profession that supplied musicians with their instruments. Musical instrument makers benefited from the general increase in musical literacy, which created more demand for musical instruments. The organization of labor in the musical instrument trade combined archaic features with more modern ones. Typically, instrument makers would be active musicians, sometimes among the best at what they did. They would follow the general trend among instrumentalists in that they tended to pass their trade on from father to son. Entire extended families could be active in the same line of work, and often their combined activities spanned a very wide geographical area. One of the families involved in lute making will provide an excellent example. The Tieffenbruckers, who originated from a small village in Bavaria, could be found in the sixteenth century in Venice, Bologna, Padua, Genoa, Lyons, and Paris, and their combined activities in this field lasted beyond the chronological boundaries of the Renaissance. It is likely that the various branches of the family kept in touch and continued to trade. The Lyons branch, for example, specialized in the production of viols, but one member of the Venetian branch was said in 1575 to be traveling regularly to "French lands" carrying several lutes at a time, and it is possible that these were sent to the French branch of the family to be sold in their shops. Another famous family of instrument makers, the Bassanos, emigrated from Italy to England, recruited by King Henry VIII for his court as musicians. Again, there is evidence that the "English" branch kept in touch with the "Italian" branch and might even have kept commercial relations and partnerships.

The organization of an instrument making workshop varied tremendously depending on the types of instruments built. Keyboard instruments, such as harpsichords, were often built in small workshop with only one owner/master builder and a couple of helpers, while lutes could be built in workshops approaching industrial size. Wind instrument makers tended not to be too specialized and made several types of instruments without necessarily concentrating on one product. In general, we can say that the overall impression we get of the musical instrument trade in the Renaissance is of a growing market spurred by the fashion for music and able to offer the most capable artisans considerable rewards.

A Contract for the Purchase and Resale of Instruments

This contract was drawn on March 30, 1559. Contracts like this one are quite rare because normal purchases of instruments did not need the drawing up of a contract. This document is really more of a partnership between instrument makers and players, with the players acting, as it were, as salespersons for the instrument makers. Notice the way in which the parties try to cover all the possible situations that might arise from the partnership.

Master Jacomo da Bassan and the said Santo, his son-in-law, commit themselves in all respects to work and manufacture all types of wind instruments for Mr. Paolo and his above-mentioned partners, of the sort and quality that the three partners will request and order; and this for a period of three consecutive years from the date of the present agreement and at the prices that will be listed below. They declare also that master Jacomo and Santo may work and make any type of said instruments for anybody else, whether he be from this city or from abroad, who will wish to have such instruments made, with the following condition, that when they make a sale to such individuals the profit in excess of the prices listed below will be divided into thirds, one third to master Jacomo and to Santo and two thirds to Mr. Paolo, Francesco and their fellow player. And if the three musicians will re-sell the instruments built and delivered to them for a price exceeding that listed below, the sum in excess shall be divided into thirds as in the previous case. Both parties shall keep truthful and honest accounts of what will be built, received, and sold, and they shall settle their accounts every six months. They also have agreed on this condition: that when instruments made for third parties, or received by the three partners, will be offered for sale, each party shall inform the other, so that one person from each side will be present at the negotiations and at the sale, in order that they be able to share the sum exceeding the fixed prices listed below. The three musicians and players solemnly promise that they will give forty ducats to master Jacomo and to Santo, so that the said society might be better prepared to manufacture said instruments. These forty ducats shall be reimbursed at the rate of four ducats a month, in the form of instruments and services that will be rendered each month to the three musicians, and this month after month.[3]

NOTES

1. *Thomas Platter's Travels in England, 1599,* translated and with introductory matter by C. Williams (London: J. Cape, 1937), 204.

2. My translation from an unpublished document in the Archivio di Stato di Venezia, Procuratori di San Marco de Supra, Decreti e Terminazioni, Reg. 135, folio 28, February 24, 1581.

3. Transcribed and translated in my article "16th-Century Venetian Wind Instrument Makers and Their Clients," *Early Music,* XIII/3 (August 1985), 397.

CHAPTER 6

Music Printing and Publishing in the Renaissance

When in the middle of the fifteenth century Johannes Gutenberg devised a method to print text from movable type, he launched a technological and cultural revolution that had profound effects on virtually all aspects of Renaissance life. It would not be an exaggeration to compare his invention of printing, and its effect on the Western European world, with the introduction of the personal computer and the availability of the World Wide Web in the late twentieth century. The printing of books made a vast treasure of theoretical and philosophical works, poetry, manuals, and religious literature available to a much larger audience than ever before. Where once scribes in a workshop, taking dictation from a master, would be able to write at most a dozen copies of a book at the same time, now a normal press run numbered somewhere between 400 and 1,200 copies, and each printed copy was cheaper and sometimes more reliable than a manuscript. Music printing did not immediately follow Gutenberg's invention: there were technical challenges, as printers had to figure out a way to print not only the note heads and stems but also the staff lines from movable type, and there were economic realities, since the market for music books was much smaller than that for books in other fields. A few examples of music printing from the fifteenth century do survive. These are most often musical examples in theoretical or liturgical books and were virtually always printed using a woodblock technique, not particularly suited to larger press runs, instead of the new technique invented by Gutenberg.

The solution to the technical problem of how to print music from movable type was found by the printer Ottaviano dei Petrucci, originally from the small city of Fossombrone in Italy. Petrucci worked in Venice, a city that had already become a major center of printing due to its flourishing trade, its lively intellectual circles, and the relatively permissive attitude of its government. In 1498 he obtained a twenty-year copyright from the Venetian government in preparation for launching his printing business. Petrucci's solution was aesthetically elegant but required extreme technical skills on the part of the printer (see illustration on p. 19). In a process known as multiple impression printing, Petrucci would print the staff lines first, then put the same piece of paper back in the press to print the notes; it is unclear whether song texts required yet a third pressing. It was essential for the paper to be carefully aligned every time it went under the press, as even a minor mistake in this area would result in unusable copies and in wasting precious and expensive paper. In his application to the Venetian government for an exclusive privilege (that is, a patent or copyright), Petrucci is justly proud of his achievement:

> Ottaviano dei Petrucci of Fossombrone, an inhabitant of this illustrious city [Venice], a very ingenious man, has, at great expense and with most watchful care, executed what many, not only in Italy but also outside of Italy, have long attempted in vain, which is, with the utmost convenience, to print Figured Music [i.e., polyphony]. And still more easily, as a result of this, Plainchant: a thing very important to the Christian religion, a great embellishment, and exceedingly necessary: wherefore the above-named petitioner seeks relief at the feet of your Most Illustrious Signory, pleading that the Signory, through its accustomed clemency and benignity, deign to accord him, as first inventor, the special grace that for twenty years no other be empowered to print Figured Music in the lands subject to Your Signory, nor tablatures for organ or lute, nor to import said things, printed outside in any other place whatsoever, nor cause them to be imported or sold in the territories or places belonging to Your Sublime Signory, on pain of confiscation of said works and a fine of ten ducats for each copy thereof.[1]

This is a remarkable document, asking for a real monopoly on music printing in one of the major printing centers of the Renaissance. Also remarkable is the punishment Petrucci proposes for the transgressors. A house for a shopkeeper or a tradesman could easily be rented for an entire year for about twenty or thirty ducats, so the penalty of ten ducats per copy could easily amount to a very large sum of money. There is no doubt that Petrucci was serious in his attempt to monopolize the market. In 1501, using his method, Petrucci printed an

Stradano, *A printing workshop.* This picture shows the various steps involved in printing a book in the Renaissance. On the left, compositors place pieces of type in trays and forms; in the center we see forms being inked prior to pressing and an assistant placing the printed sheets on a pile, while a proofreader checks one printed sheet. On the right, we can see the printing press. (Courtesy of Giraudon, Art Resource.)

anthology of fashionable French songs and, in a clear homage to current intellectual trends, he gave it a title derived from Greek, *Odhecaton*, that is, "one hundred songs," even though the collection included only 96 titles. Between 1501 and 1509 Petrucci managed to print about forty music books, including many collections of Italian *frottole* and several books of music from the composer Josquin Desprez. Although his publications were popular and set a high technical standard for the sixteenth century, Petrucci was not successful as a businessman and was forced to move from Venice after 1509. This might have been due to political events, as the War of the League of Cambrai brought misery to northern Italy and, in particular, to Venice, which for a while lost all of her mainland possessions. Such a situation was not conducive to the trade on which a business like music printing was highly dependent. There was simply no way that a printed music book could sell all of the press run, no matter how limited, within the boundaries of a single city, even a music-loving and prosperous city such as Venice, and the restrictions imposed by the war were forcing many businessmen into closing their businesses, if not into bankruptcy. The technical demands of Petrucci's method might have contributed to his difficulties, since it was essential for him to employ only highly skilled workers, some of whom would have had to be knowledgeable in musical notation, another specialized skill.

If Petrucci is the pioneer of music printing, the invention of the method that really made possible a veritable explosion in the volume of music books of the sixteenth century was accomplished by a French printer, Pierre Attaingnant, who worked in Paris. Attaingnant realized that if he treated every single note on the page as a single piece of type and put on his fonts not just the note head but also short segments of staff lines, he could simply use the same printing method (single impression printing) by which all other books were published. In his process a compositor would stand in front of a case full of type, picking up the appropriate notes one by one from a series of bins and arranging them on his composing stick roughly in the way that one arranges the tiles on the holder while playing Scrabble. Each line of type was then put into a form, and when a page was completed the form would be tightened, inked, and pressed against a sheet of paper in the press. There were slight drawbacks, since the printer did not have just a single piece of type for a whole note but a bin of types for whole notes on the first line of the staff (which when used upside down would yield whole notes on the fifth line), one for whole notes on the first space, and so on. The overall appearance of such a print could never match the elegance of those of Petrucci, but there were great advantages in speed and ease of preparation, which, of course made the printing of music much cheaper.

Shortly after his discovery of this process, Attaingnant applied for a "privilege" to cover the contents of his books, which the French king quickly granted. This was routinely done to make sure that others could not benefit by pirating editions. Only a few years later, King Francis I expanded this privilege and granted Attaingnant a virtual monopoly in music printing in France: "We will and ordain that for the time and term of six years to follow, starting with the date of the present day, none other than the said suppliant or those having charge from him, may print or put up for sale the said books and quires of music in compositions and tablatures for the playing of lutes, flutes and organs declared above."[2] Attaingnant took advantage of the popularity of the French chansons of the period and printed several books of this repertory, starting in 1527. His books were widely circulated all over Europe and imitators cropped up almost immediately, capitalizing on the potential for this new invention. By the middle of the century several cities had established themselves as music printing centers, first among them Venice (in part on the strength of the contribution of an immigrant French printer, Antonio Gardano), Lyons, Paris, Antwerp, and Nuremberg. Most of the cities with flourishing musical printing presses had a lively trade and established trade routes, which made the distribution of books across Europe much easier. Venice, for example, had regular shipping routes extending to the English Channel, exporting luxury goods to England and the northern European ports. By the 1540s and 1550s the music printing trade was well established and books began to pour forth from presses.

Collectors had begun to assemble music libraries almost from the very beginning of the history of music printing. One of the best known among them was Ferdinand Columbus, the son of Christopher Columbus, whose library still survives (minus some losses sustained during the intervening centuries) as the Biblioteca Colombina in Seville, Spain. Columbus, with the true spirit of a collector, kept meticulous records, which still survive, tracking the acquisition of music books that commercial agents bought for him in Italy, recording the place where they were purchased, the purchase price, and other bibliographic details.

Although Columbus was unique in the maniacal precision of his records, many other private collectors in the sixteenth century assembled sizable libraries that have formed the core of several famous music libraries in Europe. Printers and publishers also brought their books to annual fairs, the most important being the Messe (Fair) in Frankfurt, a book fair still held today. We know that Italian publishers, for example, would engage the services of traveling salesmen who would pack the books in barrels for the long trip on horseback across the Alps on their way to Frankfurt. Once at the fair, books would be sold to other book dealers who took them to a wide variety of final destinations. It would be easy to think of the sixteenth century as a time when travel and commercial exchanges were extraordinarily difficult, but, in fact, within the technological limitations of the time, commercial exchanges of this type occurred on a rather large scale, and music books and instruments crisscrossed the continent on their way from producers to consumers.

Amateurs and professionals alike now had access to a much broader repertory than ever before. Although music publications were not very cheap, they were at least affordable for a relatively large segment of the music-loving public. Publishers and musicians soon became aware of the commercial potential and implications of music printing, something that changed the landscape of music within a few decades of the introduction of the music printing process. Among the results of this realization was the discovery of the power of marketing. The most elaborate manuscripts in which music circulated before the sixteenth century were often commissioned by patrons, and the scribes, in effect, knew before even finishing their work that the manuscript would be bought at a fair price. These manuscripts often contained elaborate illuminations and were copied with great care. The more "everyday" manuscripts were often copied by the musicians themselves for very utilitarian purposes, that is, to remember a favorite piece of music, to send a copy of one's own composition to a patron or a friend, or to study a master's composition. There was no real need to make any efforts at reaching a wider audience or to stimulate sales. All this changed when music printing made its appearance. Essentially, by the middle of the sixteenth century, music publishers produced two types of music prints. One was what we might call a "vanity" print: a composer, usually an amateur, would draw a contract with a printer, financing the complete cost of the enterprise, and receive from the printer all the copies of the completed work. In this arrangement there was absolutely no risk for the printer who was paid in advance, independently of the commercial success of the print. On the other hand, a printer or publisher could shoulder part (or all) of the financial risks if he thought that there was a demand for the music; naturally, he would be hoping to recoup the investment with the volume of sales.

The following is an example of a printing contract of 1565. Few printing contracts for music books are preserved from the earliest period of music printing. This is an agreement that does not entail any risks for the printer. The monastery of S. Giorgio agrees to pay for all expenses and to receive all books. The printer is paid whether such books are resold or not. Many of the printed music collections of the time were probably published with similar arrangements.

8 March 1565

I, Don Benedetto, Venetian, monk of S. Giorgio in Venice, as agent for said monastery promise to give to Mr. Girolamo Scotto 88 ducats and 5 lire when said Mr. Girolamo will give me five hundred copies of the music of Don Paolo from Ferrara, printed in good size type, on regular paper, without errors, according to the original copy, printed at the expenses of the printer, with the understanding that the regular paper must be white and nice, not dark or full of stains, and that the musical notes be in the right places according to the original copy that I will give him. If by any chance some sheets will have mistakes, I want Mr. Girolamo to be responsible for reprinting them at his expenses. In addition, I want that at least a sheet a day be printed and that this project should begin next Monday. And if said Mr. Girolamo will be found wanting in any of the things outlined above, I want this contract to be null and void, and so that it be known that Mr. Girolamo freely agrees to do the things I have written above, he will sign this of his own hand, and he will write his own copy of the contract, which I will sign. I, Girolamo Scotto, am satisfied and I agree to what is written above, and without any other legal document, I am satisfied.

[Added:] 10 June 1565. The above-mentioned Mr. Girolamo Scotto has given to Don Benedetto according to the terms of the present contract, five hundred [music] books, which are now stored in our monastery.[3]

As the production of music prints increased, it became obvious that the buying public had to be enticed to buy a particular print out of the variety of choices available. The very first music prints essentially copied the format of music manuscripts and that meant that their title page often offered pretty plain titles. As we have seen earlier, the very first book printed from movable type had the rather uninspiring title of *Odhecathon* (One hundred songs), and many other collections of the time had descriptive titles of this type, such as "First book of madrigals" or "Second book of chansons." By the middle of the century, however, publishers had realized that a well-crafted title could play a major role in encouraging the customer to buy a particular book. Titles such as "Celestial harmony," "The sweet and harmonious concerts," "The first book of eternal motets," "The amorous concerts," and "Music of the virtuosos of the florid chapel of the most excellent Lord the Duke of Bavaria" were obviously meant to stimulate the interest of potential buyers. Also meant to entice were the numerous protestations on the title page of almost every book that the musical pieces had been "newly corrected," "now revised and corrected by the author," "newly collected and never before published," "purged of the many errors seen in previous editions," "reprinted and corrected with all possible diligence," together with fulsome claims that they were "full of every musical sweetness and beauty, and composed with a learned art," "delightful music and pleasurable to sing," or that "the beauty, quality, and charm of these madrigals will be obvious when they are sung." In a business quickly becoming more crowded with music editions, it was essential to advertise one's publications in a way that would make them stand out from the rest.

Sometimes publishers used a bit of creative license in their title page claims, for example, by placing the name of a famous composer prominently on the title page, even though the majority of the composition in the publication might be by a lesser known musician. The record in this case might belong to the French publisher Antonio Gardano, who worked in Venice. In 1541 Gardano published a collection of three-voice madrigals whose title page highlighted the name of the popular composer Costanzo Festa: only one of the compositions included in the volume, however, was really by Festa.

Composers were not slow to realize the commercial possibilities of the new medium, and they began to pay more attention to it. Often they personally supervised the work of the printer, not only to make sure that the edition would be of the highest quality but also in order to include new works not yet available to the general public (a fact that was usually advertised on the title page). Sometimes composers and musicians took on the role of music editors, collecting pieces from colleagues and friends, and arranging them in an anthology with clear commercial purposes. In short, the advent of music printing offered musicians a direct avenue to the public and the possibility to realize some not insignificant income.

Patrons and employers of musicians were initially wary of allowing music composed for their enjoyment to be made available to larger audiences. A famous letter from 1544 describes the attitude of a noble patron: "This Mr. Neri spends hundred of ducats a year in this endeavor [music making], and he keeps [the music] to himself; not even for his own father would he part with a song."[4] We know of many cases where music composed by musicians in the service of a ruler was guarded jealously during his reign and released only after his death. Patrons, not unreasonably, felt that music composed for their use by musicians in their employment became, as it were, their own property in the same way that a painting or a sculpture would. Often this attitude stemmed from the knowledge that certain pieces of music contained new developments that a patron wanted to keep to himself in order to impress his guests and friends. Slowly, though, patrons began to take pride in the widespread fame and recognition that their composers could gain on an international stage by publishing their best works; in fact, at times the aristocracy took advantage of the printing medium by releasing detailed descriptions complete with musical editions of the court entertainments organized for important events, such as dynastic marriages or state visits. In other words, they realized that, in the right circumstances, the diffusion of the musical repertory of their court, far from being a liability, would enhance their status as patrons of culture and the arts, a fact that would more than balance the loss of exclusive enjoyment of the music.

One other possibly unintended effect of the invention of music printing was the change in the attitude toward "old" music, at least as far as some musical genres are concerned. Around 1473 the theorist Johannes Tinctoris could confidently state: "In addition, it is a matter of great surprise that there is no composition written over forty years ago which is thought by the learned to be worthy of performance."[5] In the sixteenth century, however, compositions that captured the public's fancy could enjoy a long life and were republished for several decades, sometimes long after the death of their composer. Thus, for example, a collection of madrigals by Arcadelt, first published in 1539, was reprinted regularly through the sixteenth century and was still available to music lovers in the 1650s. This phenomenon was fueled by an increase in musical literacy that had no precedent in Western Europe. Singing of secular music at social gathering became desirable, but not all amateurs had the musical skills to keep up with increasingly difficult compositions as the century progressed. Thus, older compositions, often much simpler from those at the cutting edge of musical development, retained a large audience, and their reprints were still highly profitable for music publishers. This does not mean that audiences did not like the latest developments; in fact, there was often an attitude that contemporary composers were producing the best music, and we even encounter some criticism of older music as being "quaint" or not as perfect and refined as the latest pieces. When the composer and organist Claudio Merulo became briefly involved in music printing, he issued in 1566 a reprint of a book of madrigals by Philippe Verdelot, an item that seems to have been in high demand throughout the century. In the preface to the collection, though, Merulo mentions that he revised and corrected these madrigals, purging them of some old-fashioned touches that he considered no longer acceptable, even though the original volume had been published less than thirty years earlier. Still, the fact that "older" music was still being heard and circulated did change the musical landscape, and it is interesting to note that in one of the most heated theoretical debates of the early seventeenth century, between the theorist Giovanni Maria Artusi and the composer Claudio Monteverdi, each side appealed to the authority of composers who had been dead for more than four decades.

Another way in which music publishing affected the musical world of the sixteenth century was by creating a demand for an ever-increasing number of manuals and treatises aimed at amateurs and professionals, often an invaluable source of information for the modern understanding of sixteenth-century music. Many of the manuals gave basic instruction in singing, playing, or dancing and were definitely meant for middle-class amateurs. Professional musicians and wealthy citizens had no great need of these works, since they received their instruction in private settings, learning from a tutor or often (in the case of professional musicians) from a close relative. Manuals made some of this information available to a much wider public. Now that some form of basic musicianship became a desirable social skill necessary for maintaining the proper status in society and for being considered educated, the socially ambitious lady or gentleman had to find ways to learn music. The markets for books of music and manuals were, of course, interconnected in that the availability of cheaper sheet music fueled the interest of a broader public, while manuals in turn made it possible for more amateurs to gain the musical skills that would make them consumers of more music books. An additional benefit for us is that, thanks to these manuals, we know much more about the musical practices of the sixteenth century than about those of any preceding period in music history. Music printing is also responsible for the fact that much more music survives from the sixteenth century than from any of the previous centuries, giving us a rather detailed knowledge of this repertory. The difference is obvious when we consider, for example, that the entire surviving repertory of fourteenth-century Italian secular music, one of the most important late medieval musical achievements, consists of a few hundred pieces. In the sixteenth century, on the other hand, the printer Ottaviano Scotto alone published almost four hundred music books, each containing several musical pieces, between 1539 and 1572. It was unavoidable that such a flood of music, and the economics behind it, would transform profoundly the way in which both consumers and producers of music operated.

NOTES

1. Translated in Gustave Reese, "The First Printed Collection of Part Music," *Musical Quarterly* 20 (1934), 40.

2. Translated in Daniel Heartz, "A New Attaingnant Book and the Beginnings of French Music Printing," *Journal of the American Musicological Society* 14/1 (Spring 1961), 22.

3. The original document is transcribed in Richard Agee, "The Privilege and Venetian Music Printing in the Sixteenth Century" (Ph.D. diss., Princeton University, 1982), 335.

4. *The Renaissance*, ed. by Gary Tomlinson, in *Source Readings in Music History*, Oliver Strunk, ed., vol. 3, rev. ed. (New York: W. W. Norton, 1998), 56.

5. Piero Weiss and Richard Taruskin, *Music in the Western World* (New York: W. W. Norton, 1984), 80.

Further Readings

Many books on the music history of a particular period might require some degree of musical literacy to understand the discussions of music included there. I have included in this list only a handful of works that include information accessible to interested readers of this book. Many more works, mostly of a more specialized nature, are of course available. I would suggest consulting the bibliographies included in each of the following works.

The most important and comprehensive reference work about music is *The New Grove Dictionary of Music and Musicians*, 29 vols., 2nd ed., ed. by Stanley Sadie. New York: Grove's Dictionaries, 2000.

For surveys of the music of the period I would recommend:

Atlas, Allan W. *Renaissance Music: Music in Western Europe, 1400–1600*. New York: Norton, 1998.

Brown, Howard Mayer, and Louise K. Stein. *Music in the Renaissance*, 2nd ed. Upper Saddle River, N.J.: Prentice Hall, 1999.

Perkins, Leeman L. *Music in the Age of the Renaissance*. New York: Norton, 1999.

Strohm, Reinhard. *The Rise of European Music, 1380–1500*. Cambridge: Cambridge University Press, 1993.

Collections of essays that are useful and accessible are:

Brown, Howard Mayer, and Stanley Sadie, eds. *Performance Practice: Music Before 1600*. New York: The Macmillan Press, 1989.

Fenlon, Iain, ed. *The Renaissance: From the 1470s to the End of the Sixteenth Century*. Englewood Cliffs, N.J.: Prentice Hall, 1989.

Knighton, Tess, and David Fallows, eds. *Companion to Medieval and Renaissance Music*. Berkeley: University of California Press, 1992.

For transcriptions and translations of contemporary documents about music, see:

Tomlinson, Gary, ed. *The Renaissance* in *Source Readings in Music History*, Oliver Strunk, ed., vol. 3, rev. ed. New York: Norton, 1998.

Weiss, Piero, and Richard Taruskin, eds. *Music in the Western World*. New York: Schirmer, 1984.

RECORDINGS

Given the amazing increase in the number of available recordings for this repertory, it is practically impossible to attempt to provide a current discography of Renaissance music. Unfortunately, the books surveying this period do not come with a set of CDs illustrating the music of the time. Broader survey textbooks often do, but the space dedicated to Renaissance music there might be somewhat limited. In addition, CDs of Renaissance music today tend to be more specialized in terms of repertory: instead of covering a broad range of styles and genres, most focus on a composer, or a particular genre in a well defined period. It might be best to inquire at a good record store with a sizable section on classical music, and to be guided by specific suggestions, depending on the type of music one might want to explore.

Biographies

ARCADELT, JACQUES (ca. 1505–1568). French or Flemish composer. He spent a great deal of his career in Italy, contributing greatly to the development of the Italian madrigal, of which he was one of the early masters. His madrigals were reprinted throughout the sixteenth century, attesting to his success. he also composed a large number of French *chansons* and a number of pieces of sacred music.

ATTAINGNANT, PIERRE (ca. 1494–1551/52). One of the most important printers of music in the sixteenth century. Attaingnant perfected a method (single impression printing) that, while not as elegant as some of the early printed music collections, was practical and easy to use. His innovations were responsible for the enormous development in music printing in the period. He was the royal printer of music from 1537 to 1547, a token of appreciation from the French crown.

BINCHOIS, GILLES (ca. 1400–1460). A Franco-Flemish composer who, together with Dufay and Dunstable, was held as model of compositional skills by his contemporaries. From the 1420s on he served the court of Burgundy, one of the most important courts of the fifteenth century. His particularly known for his secular compositions, in the genre we now call the "Burgundian chanson," which he infused with his own distinctive melancholy.

BUSNOIS, ANTOINE (ca. 1430–1492). After possibly spending some time as a pupil of Johannes Ockeghem, Busnois joined the chapel of the court of Burgundy, serving there until 1482. He then moved to Bruges, where he remained until his death. Busnois is an important link between the early and late periods of the fifteenth century: although he left several sacred compositions, he is at his best in the *chanson*.

BYRD, WILLIAM (1543–1623). After an early stint at Lincoln Cathedral, this English composer joined the Chapel Royal of the court of Queen Elizabeth, quickly becoming one of the favorite composers of the Queen. In Protestant England, Byrd chose to remain Catholic, but—likely because of the protection of the Queen—he does not seem to have suffered because of it. Byrd was an extremely versatile composer, equally at ease in sacred and secular music, and writing for the voice or for instruments. Many influential English composers of the time were his pupils.

CARA, MARCO (or Marchetto) (ca. 1470–1525). Italian composer. With Bartolomeo Tromboncino, Cara was responsible for establishing the genre of the *frottola*—writing more than 100 of these secular songs. He served most of his life at the court of Mantua, enjoying the favor of Isabella d'Este, the spouse of the ruling duke, a woman famous for her love and support of music.

CLEMENS (non Papa), JACOB (ca. 1510–1555). Franco-Flemish composer, among the most prolific of his generation. Clemens wrote more than 200 motets and several mass cycles, using a distinctive style based on prevalence of imitative counterpoint. He also wrote a large collection of simple settings of the Psalms in Dutch. He might have served the Emperor Charles V for a while, but most of his life was spent in the service of several churches in the Low Lands.

DESPREZ, JOSQUIN (ca. 1450–1521). Josquin is without a doubt the most famous composer of his generation, praised by contemporaries and followers. His popularity was helped by the fact that the first printer of polyphonic music from movable type, Ottaviano Petrucci, chose several of Josquin's compositions for publication. Among others, Martin Luther praised Josquin lavishly, singling him out among his contemporaries. Josquin served for many years in Italy, but he also spent large parts of his career in France, particularly the last years of his life. Josquin composed music in a wide variety of genres, both secular and sacred. He is known for the clarity of his organization, for his variety in texture, his memorable vocal lines, and the attention he paid to the setting of the text.

DOWLAND, JOHN (1563–1626). English composer and lutenist. Dowland was one of the best lute players of his day and held several posts both in England (eventually becoming court lutenist in 1612) and at the court of Denmark, where he also acted as a spy for the English crown. He is best known for his secular songs, often full of feeling and pathos, with a slightly dark bent, and for his instrumental compositions, which were often used by others for arrangements and variations.

DUFAY, GUILLAUME (ca. 1398–1474). The foremost composer of his generation, praised and honored by his contemporaries and followers. Dufay was born in France and trained in Cambrai. In the early 1420s he moved to Italy, first serving local courts and later singing in the papal choir. While in the service of the pope, Dufay composed one of the most famous pieces of the Renaissance to celebrate the dedication of the cathedral of Florence, a ceremony in which the pope (and his choir) took part. He spent the later part of his life in Cambrai, where he had obtained the position of canon of the cathedral. Dufay was equally at ease in all types of music cultivated in his time, both secular and sacred, and was extremely important in the development of a Renaissance musical language.

DUNSTABLE, JOHN (ca. 1390–1453). English composer, mathematician, court official, and astronomer, so important in the music of this time that a later theorist called him "the source and origin" of all later music. Dunstable was active in England and on the continent, where he followed his master, the Duke of Bedford. His works were widely copied in continental manuscripts, showing that his music was very popular. His style, which was often praised for its "sweetness," gives a sound more full and refined than that of his predecessors. Dunstable also shows a great amount of interest in setting the text appropriately. Most of his music was composed for the church.

FESTA, COSTANZO (ca. 1490–1545). Italian composer and singer, one of the "founding fathers" of the Italian madrigal. Festa sang in the papal choir in Rome, and composed a fair amount of sacred music, which was widely circulated, but his fame rests on his madrigals, which were published between 1530 and 1549 in several collections of the time.

FRANCESCO CANOVA DA MILANO (1497–1543). Italian lute virtuoso and composer. He served several important patrons as instrumentalist, and was renowned for his performances on his favorite instrument, the lute. Francesco was extremely influential in the growth of instrumental music in the sixteenth century, both as a performer and as a composer. He was the first Italian composer of the Renaissance to achieve widespread fame in Europe.

GABRIELI, ANDREA (1533–1585). Italian organist and composer. After holding some minor posts, Gabrieli was hired in 1566 to the post of organist in the church of St. Mark's in Venice, where he remained until his death. His importance as a composer is tied to his sacred music, written in a newer, majestic style that matched the grandeur of the ceremonial occasions for which it was intended. Gabrieli influenced a number of composers, especially those of the so-called Venetian School.

GABRIELI, GIOVANNI (ca. 1553/56–1612). Italian organist and composer, nephew of Andrea Gabrieli. Giovanni followed in his uncle's footsteps and served at St. Mark's from 1585 to his death. His compositions also followed and refined his uncle's innovations. Giovanni is famous for large-scale pieces combining voices and instruments, and for his influential instrumental compositions. His influence was widespread, since he taught a number of younger contemporaries, both Italians and foreigners.

GESUALDO, CARLO, PRINCE OF VENOSA (ca. 1561–1613). Italian composer. Gesualdo was not a professional musician but a high-ranking nobleman from an important family who had a great passion for music. He is notorious for killing his first wife, whom he found with her lover (a situation that justified the crime at the time). His music, especially his madrigals, continues to be famous for its unexpected harmonies, with an unusual amount of dissonances. The fact that Gesualdo did not depend on music for his livelihood might have been a factor in his use of "experimental" techniques.

GLAREANUS, HEINRICH (1488–1563). Swiss scholar, poet, and music theorist. Glareanus was in contact with numerous humanists, most notably Erasmus, and also with many composers and musicians of this time. In 1547 he published one of the most important Renaissance books on music theory, the *Dodecachordon* [from the Greek for having twelve strings], whose title refers to his new division of harmony into twelve modes, not eight as it was previously done. Glareanus was a great admirer of the music of Josquin Desprez, whose works are often found in his book as musical examples. The *Dodecachordon* influenced successive generations of musicians and music theorists.

GOMBERT, NICOLAS (ca. 1495–1560). Flemish composer and singer. From 1526 he served in the choir of the Emperor Charles V and traveled widely. Dismissed from his service around 1540 and sent to the galleys for some serious misconduct, he was later pardoned by the Emperor it was said after presenting a particularly fine set of compositions to the monarch. His music, especially that of his motets, is one of the best expressions of the style of the generation of composers that followed Josquin Desprez. His skillful use of imitation was a model for his contemporaries.

ISAAC, HEINRICH (ca. 1450–1517). Flemish composer, contemporary of Josquin. Isaac sang in Florence, where he enjoyed the protection of the Medici family, in particular of Lorenzo the Magnificent. After the (temporary) end to the Medici rule, Isaac was hired by the Emperor Maximilian I as "court composer," probably the first instance of a musician hired exclusively for his composing skills. Later in his life he returned to Florence, where he died. Isaac composed in a variety of styles, both in his secular and sacred music, ranging from simple carnival songs to some of the most complex polyphonic pieces of the period. In some of his compositions he seems to have been influenced by the Italian taste for clear and proper text setting.

JANEQUIN, CLÉMENT (ca. 1485–1558). French composer. In 1549 he settled in Paris, finally being appointed royal composer. His fame rests on his musical settings of French secular songs, those of the so-called "Parisian chanson," which often contain re-creations of soundscapes (e.g., "The battle," "The songs of the birds," "The market cries of Paris"). His "battle" pieces, in particular, were famous all over Europe and were often reworked and arranged.

LASSO, ORLANDO DI (ca. 1530–1594). Composer and singer. Lasso as a youth was prized for the beauty of his voice. Most of his career, after an extended stay in Italy, was spent at the court of the Dukes of Bavaria in Munich, where he served Albrecht V and his son Wilhelm V from 1556 until his death. After 1563 he was the director of the chapel and, thus, presided over one of the most important and largest musical establishments of the time. His works were published with great success and brought him an international reputation. Lasso was one of the most cosmopolitan composers of the Renaissance, equally at ease in French chansons, Italian madrigals, German songs, and sacred music and employing a variety of styles, always with a keen ear for the correct text setting. He was also a very prolific composer, leaving behind almost 2,000 works.

MARENZIO, LUCA (1553/54–1599). Italian composer. Born in Northern Italy, he made his way to Rome around 1574 and spent most of his life there, in the service of many aristocrats and cardinals. Marenzio was one of the most famous (and prolific) madrigal composers of his time, and his music was admired and imitated as far away as England.

MONTE, PHILIPPE DE (1521–1603). Flemish composer and singer. Much of his earlier career was spent abroad, most notably in Italy and in England. In 1568, while he was in Rome, he was called to Vienna, where he was appointed Kappellmeister (director of the chapel) at the Imperial court, a post he retained until his death. He composed both sacred and secular music, but his production in the madrigal field (well over a thousand compositions) was mostly responsible for his success and fame.

MONTEVERDI, CLAUDIO (1567–1643). Italian composer. Monteverdi spent almost all his creative life between Mantua and Venice. The last thirty years of his life were spent as director of music at St. Mark's, in Venice, where he composed sacred music and also contributed important works to the operatic stage. Although most of his music falls under the early Baroque period, his early polyphonic madrigals are perhaps the finest, last expression of this Renaissance genre.

MOUTON, JEAN (before 1459–1522). French composer and singer. Contrary to the prevailing trends of the day, Mouton did not seek employment outside of his native country, culminating his career by joining the musical establishment of the French court in 1502 and remaining there until his death. He is most famous for his motets, of which over 100 survive. His music is characterized by superior technical ability and by clear, flowing motives.

OBRECHT, JACOB (ca. 1450–1505). Netherlandish composer and singer. Among the most important composers of his generation, Obrecht worked mainly in the region close to his native city. Later in life, after he had been recognized by many as one of the outstanding composer of the time, he also traveled to Italy. During a visit to Ferrara, Italy, he died during an outbreak of the plague. He is mostly famous for his sacred music, in which he showed the typical Northern European taste for complex technical solutions, but his music never fails to sound full and satisfying.

OCKEGHEM, JOHANNES (ca. 1410–1497). One of the most important composers of the fifteenth century, with a long-standing connection to the French royal court, where he served from 1451 on (although not without some interruptions for trips abroad). Ockeghem's surviving music is relatively little for someone with such a long career, suggesting much might have been lost. Many of his surviving pieces are characterized by an intense exploration of technical challenges and are often cited by theorists as example of technical virtuosity. His polyphonic setting of the *Requiem*, the Mass for the Dead, is the earliest in the history of music.

PALESTRINA, GIOVANNI PIERLUIGI DA (1525/26–1594). Italian composer and singer. Palestrina spent virtually all of his life in Rome, serving at some of the most important churches. From 1571 until his death he worked as chapelmaster at the Cappella Giulia, the choir of the basilica of St. Peter's, in Rome. Palestrina is perhaps the earliest composer whose style survived long after his death, and was held up as a model of Catholic choral music. Many anecdotes and stories (many of which are inaccurate or false) circulated about this master and helped sustain his fame through the centuries. His sacred music is the epitome of Catholic church music of the late sixteenth century, characterized by a smooth texture and melodic lines, and the avoidance of the most progressive traits found in the music of other composers.

PETRUCCI, OTTAVIANO DEI (1466–1539). Italian music printer. In the 1490s he moved to Venice, then a flourishing center for the new printing industry, and in a few years he invented a system to print polyphonic music from movable type. His first collection, the *Odhecaton* of 1501, included 96 pieces of secular music. He followed that effort with a series of volumes, thus launching the music publishing industry in Europe. The books of Petrucci are extremely elegant, but his rather complicated printing system was superseded by the one developed by the French printer Pierre Attaingnant.

POWER, LEONEL (d. 1445). English composer. Power, unlike his contemporary and fellow countryman Dunstable, seems to have worked his entire life in England. With Dunstable, he is credited with the development of a new style of sacred music that was quickly imitated by the continental composers, who dubbed it "the English manner." His production is confined to sacred music, and he might have been at least partly responsible for the copying of the so-called Old

Hall Manuscript, the most important collection of English sacred music of the time.

RORE, CIPRIANO DE (1515/16–1565). Flemish composer. Rore spent a considerable part of his life in Italy, but his career seems characterized by a certain amount of restlessness, which pushed him to seek frequent changes of employment, for example at Ferrara, Parma, and Venice. Rore was a consummate master of sacred and secular music: his madrigals are his most important contribution. Rore was the first to elevate the madrigal to a level of artistic expression that made it the favorite of music lovers for the remainder of the century. His stark, deeply felt settings of the poetry of Petrarch were extremely influential.

SENFL, LUDWIG (ca. 1486–1542/43). Swiss composer. Senfl spent all of his life in German-speaking lands, working in Vienna, where he might have studied with Isaac, Augsburg, and Munich, where he stayed from 1523 on. Although he wrote a fair amount of important sacred music, Senfl is best known for his settings of German songs (Lieder), which mix a fresh, immediate poetic expression with music that often hides well its internal complexity.

SERMISY, CLAUDIN DE (ca. 1490–1562). French composer. Sermisy spent almost all of his career in the service of the French kings. His sacred music is somewhat conservative, perhaps closer to that of the previous generation, but his French songs (about 175 survive) were rightly famous for their simple, tuneful style. With Clément Janequin, he is the master of the Parisian chanson of the time.

TALLIS, THOMAS (ca. 1505–1585). English composer and organist. By 1543 Tallis was a Gentleman of the Chapel Royal in London, that is, a member of the musical establishment of the English court, a post he maintained until his death. In 1575 he and William Byrd obtained a virtual monopoly on music publishing in England from Queen Elizabeth I and, thus, were responsible for the belated flowering of music printing experienced on the island. The sacred music of Tallis is particularly important: he worked at a transitional time, and therefore wrote music in different styles, both for Catholic services and for the new Anglican liturgy. He helped establish the English anthem as the primary form of Anglican sacred music.

TAVERNER, JOHN (ca. 1490–1545). English composer, among the most influential of his generation. Taverner worked at several posts, most notably at Christ Church, Oxford. Most of his surviving music is sacred and shows an effort at combining elements of the English style of his predecessors with the new stylistic innovations of the continent, especially those seen in the music of Josquin Desprez.

TINCTORIS, JOHANNES (ca. 1435–1511). Flemish theorist and composer. Tinctoris worked both in France and in Italy, serving King Ferdinand I of Naples. Although he was also known as a composer, his fame rests on his theoretical works, arguably the most important of the late fifteenth century. Tinctoris wrote the earliest music dictionary to be printed, and compiled treatises dealing with the most important theoretical questions of his day.

TROMBONCINO, BARTOLOMEO (ca. 1470–ca. 1535). Italian singer and composer. All of Tromboncino's career was spent in northern Italy, between the courts of Mantua and Ferrara and the Republic of Venice. Together with Marco Cara, Tromboncino established the genre of the *frottola*, a light-hearted Italian song, which dominated the Italian secular music landscape of the time. Later in his career he also turned to the settings of more serious texts, but his influence declined as the Italian madrigal supplanted the *frottola* as the main Italian secular genre.

VERDELOT, PHILIPPE (ca. 1470–80?–before 1552). French composer. Trained in the Northern European tradition, by the 1520s he had moved to Italy, where he worked in Florence and Rome. Verdelot was well known in the sixteenth century both for his sacred and secular music: some of his pieces were among those most frequently reprinted by music publishers. Even though he was a Frenchman, Verdelot is perhaps best known to us for being one of the earliest masters of the Italian madrigal. His works in this genre helped launch the popularity of the madrigal and were widely circulated.

VICTORIA, TOMÁS LUIS DE (1548–1611). Spanish singer and composer. Victoria is one of the giants of Catholic sacred music in the late sixteenth century. He spent a major part of his career in Rome, holding several posts and coming into contact with many of the major composer of Catholic church music of the time, including Palestrina. In the 1580s he returned to his native Spain, where he was under the patronage of the imperial family. Victoria concentrated on Latin church music for the Catholic church (masses and motets) and, unlike most of the composers of his day, does not seem to have written secular music at all. Although he wrote in a style similar to that of Palestrina, Victoria often injects more emotional responses to the text in his music.

WERT, GIACHES DE (1535–1596). Flemish composer. Wert came to Italy early in his life, and spent more than thirty years in service of the ruling family in Mantua, the Gonzagas, who had one of the most lavish musical establishment of the period. He served as director of music for the ducal church of Santa Barbara, newly built by the Gonzagas, for many years, and composed more than 150 pieces of sacred music. However, Wert was even more famous for his production of Italian madrigals (more than 200 survive), which reflected the latest trends in musical style of the time and in the choice of texts. He was a great influence on the acknowledged master of the following generation, Claudio Monteverdi, who also worked at the court in Mantua in the 1590s and was therefore in direct contact with Wert.

WILLAERT, ADRIAN (ca. 1490–1562). Flemish composer. Willaert studied music and law in Paris, but by 1515 he had moved to Italy, serving the Este family, the rulers of Ferrara (a connection he kept for most of his life). In 1527 Willaert was appointed to the post of director of music for the church of St. Mark's in Venice, where he remained until his death. During the tenure of Willaert, St. Mark's became a major musical center; Willaert was the teacher of a generation of composers, and his opinion on musical matters was often solicited from theorists and musicians. He was equally at ease in sacred and secular music, writing important works for the church and very influential madrigals and other genres. His collection *Musica nova* ("New music"), published late in his career, is one of the most important of the sixteenth century.

ZARLINO, GIOSEFFO (1517–1590). Italian composer and theorist. After his early career at Chioggia, a small town on the edge of the Venetian lagoon, Zarlino moved to Venice in the early 1540s, studying with Willaert and later succeeding him as director of music at St. Mark's. Zarlino is not particularly distinguished as composer, but he is perhaps the most important theorist of his generation. Zarlino published a series of treatises that often use the music of his teacher Willaert as model for musical composition.

Index

Canzonet, 86
Capriccio, 97
Cara, Marco, composer, 76–77
Carnival, 131–32
Castiglione, Baldessare, writer, 49, 93, 109, 156
Castrati, 20
Catholic Church: Papal Schism, 11; music for, 122–26
Cellini, Benvenuto, 57–58
Certon, Pierre, composer, 88
Chanson, 56, 74–75; Parisian, 87–89;
Charles V, Emperor, 108, 168
Choirboys, 20, 52
Choirmaster, duties of, 120–21
Chorales, Lutheran, 128
Church choirs: duties of, 53–54; size, 119
Cittern, 160–61
Coclico, Adrianus Petit, theorist, 140
Columbus, Ferdinand, 177
Commedia dell'arte, 145
Composers, professionalization of, 45–46
Conducting in Renaissance music, 120
Confraternities, 133, 134–37
Consonance, 26–27
Consort (musical ensemble), 150
Constantinople: fall to Ottoman Turks, 2; effects of fall on European culture, 7; reaction to fall, 113
Cornetto, 163
Coryat, Thomas, traveler, 136
Council of Trent, 53, 125–26
Counter-Reformation, 125
Courtesans, 63–64
Courtly love, 74
Courts, music at, 106–16
Courville, Joachim Thibault de, 137, 139

Crumhorn, 167
Curtal, 166

Da Milano, Francesco Canova, lutenist and composer, 98–99
Dancing, in the fifteenth century, 90; in the sixteenth century, 92–95; for lower classes, 105; as part of a wedding ceremony, 111–12
de la Marche, Olivier, chronicler, 113–14
Della Casa, Giovanni, author, 9–10
Descartes de Ventemille, Jacques, writer, 98–99
Desprez, Josquin, composer, 18, 23–24, 140; *Ave Maria* (motet), 30, 33
Dialogue About Music (A. Doni), 144
Dissonance, 26–27
Donato, Baldissera, composer and singer, 121
Doni, Antonfrancesco, 144
Dowland, John, lutenist and composer, 86–87; *Flow, my tears* (lute song), 87
Dufay, Guillaume, composer, 55–56, 122, 131; *L'homme armé Mass*, 29, 32–33; *Donnes l'assault* (chanson), 75
Dunstable, John, composer, 3, 45–46, 55; *O quam pulcra es* (motet), 29, 32
Dynamics in Renaissance music, 36

Elizabeth I, Queen of England, 60, 62, 130, 154; and dancing, 115
Encina, Juan del, composer, 78
Ensalada, 78
Este, Alfonso d', Duke of Ferrara, 109

Faenza Codex, 92

Popular music in the Renaissance, 40–43, 101–6, 132; and magic, 104
Population growth in Europe, 10
Power, Leonel, composer, 3
Praetorius, Michael, composer and theorist, 151
Private music making, 141–44
Processions, 133–34

Racket (musical instrument), 166–67
Rauschpfeife (musical instrument), 167
Recorder, 163–64
Reformation, effects on music, 126–30
Regola rubertina (S. Ganassi), 156
Renaissance: chronological boundaries in music, 2–3; social developments, 9–11; population growth, 10
Rhythm in Renaissance music, 16–17
Ricercare, 96
Romance (Spanish song), 25, 78
Rome, sack of, 6
Rommelpot (musical instrument), 168
Rondeau, musical form, 75
Rore, Cipriano de, composer, 83
Ruzzante, Angelo Beolco, known as, 11

Sackbut, 162
Sanudo, Marin, diarist, 112
Savonarola, Girolamo, religious reformer, 132
Scotto, Ottaviano, music printer, 183
Senfl, Ludwig, composer, 79
Sermisy, Claudin de, composer, 88
Serpent (musical instrument), 163

Shawm, 165
Singers, 20–21, 50–57, 104
Slide trumpet, 162
Sonata, 97
Song of Songs, 32, 68, 134
Syntagma musicum (M. Praetorius), 151

Tallis, Thomas, composer, 69
Tasso, Torquato, poet, *Jerusalem delivered,* 82
Teaching (music), 61
Tempo in Renaissance music, 17, 36
Tenorlied, 42, 79
Text setting in music, 38–40, 73, 82
Texture in Renaissance music, 22–26,
Theater, and music, 145–46
Tieffenbrucker family, instrument makers, 61, 169
Tinctoris, Johannes, music theorist, 3, 46, 181
Titian, painter, 45
Toccata, 96
The Triumphs of Oriana (T. Morley), 85
Tromboncino, Bartolomeo, composer, 76
Trombone, 162
Trumpet, 161–62
"Twinkle, Twinkle, Little Star," 31

Universities, 139–41

Variation form, 97–98
Venice, 5, 52, 133–34
Verdelot, Philippe, composer, 83, 182
Vespers (religious service), 54
Vicentino, Nicola, theorist and composer, 137

About the Author

GIULIO ONGARO is Associate Professor of Music History and Literature at the Thornton School of Music, University of Southern California.